Sails Literacy Series
Teacher's Resource Book

First Wave: Beginning Level

Jill Eggleton and Jo Windsor

Contents

The *Sails Literacy Series* *First Wave: Beginning Level*

The *Sails Literacy Series* *First Wave: Beginning Level*

Introduction

The environment in which a child lives is dominated by a variety of language forms. Throughout the *First Wave: Beginning Level* series of books, children will engage with, and enjoy language in all of its variety, as they meet stories that will entertain them and drive their imagination on the initial pathway to literacy.

The *First Wave: Beginning Level* books provide opportunities for children to:

- practice the oral, written, and visual forms of language
- think critically about messages from visual sources

Throughout these books, children are encouraged to orally retell a storyline from the explicit narrative within the visuals. This oral retelling enables them to use a wider and richer vocabulary of a more complex structure than can be provided for in the written text at this stage of reading development. It supports and strengthens all language-learning areas.

The man got a banana out of the hat. Then he ate it. But he was naughty and threw away the skin. Then he slipped on it.

The *First Wave: Beginning Level* books also provide opportunities for children to learn and practice high-frequency words — words that they need to quickly and automatically recognize and differentiate from other words in order to begin their independent reading journey.

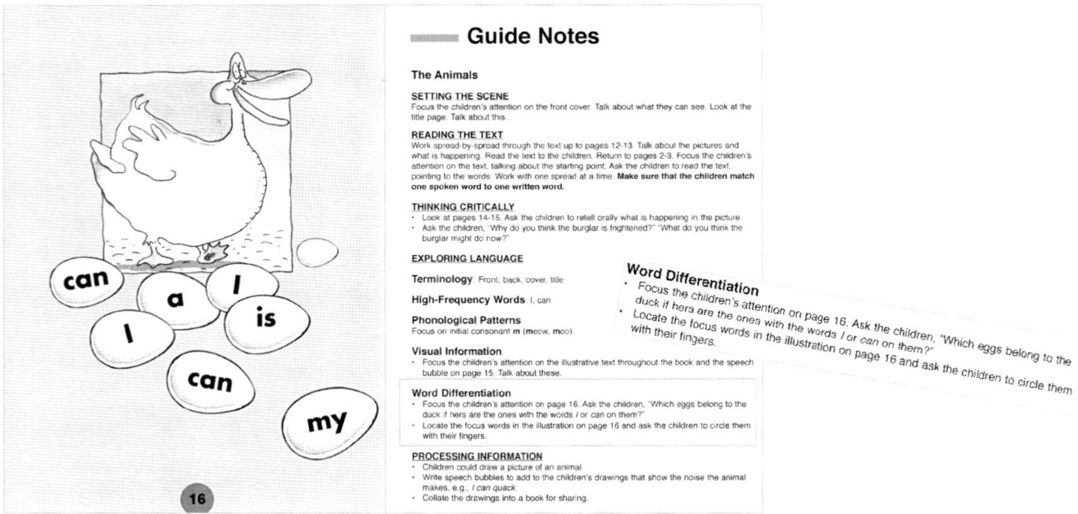

Guide Notes

The Animals

SETTING THE SCENE
Focus the children's attention on the front cover. Talk about what they can see. Look at the title page. Talk about this.

READING THE TEXT
Work spread-by-spread through the text up to pages 12-13. Talk about the pictures and what is happening. Read the text to the children. Return to pages 2-3. Focus the children's attention on the text, talking about the starting point. Ask the children to read the text, pointing to the words. Work with one spread at a time. **Make sure that the children match one spoken word to one written word.**

THINKING CRITICALLY
- Look at pages 14-15. Ask the children to retell orally what is happening in the picture.
- Ask the children, "Why do you think the burglar is frightened?" "What do you think the burglar might do now?"

EXPLORING LANGUAGE

Terminology: Front, back, cover, title

High-Frequency Words: I, can

Phonological Patterns
Focus on initial consonant **m** (**m**eow, **m**oo)

Visual Information
- Focus the children's attention on the illustrative text throughout the book and the speech bubble on page 15. Talk about these.

Word Differentiation
- Focus the children's attention on page 16. Ask the children, "Which eggs belong to the duck if hers are the ones with the words *I* or *can* on them?"
- Locate the focus words in the illustration on page 16 and ask the children to circle them with their fingers.

PROCESSING INFORMATION
- Children could draw a picture of an animal.
- Write speech bubbles to add to the children's drawings that show the noise the animal makes, e.g., *I can quack*.
- Collate the drawings into a book for sharing.

Word Differentiation
- Focus the children's attention on page 16. Ask the children, "Which eggs belong to the duck if hers are the ones with the words *I* or *can* on them?"
- Locate the focus words in the illustration on page 16 and ask the children to circle them with their fingers.

Ideas for supporting the learner in the introductory stages of processing information are provided in the **Guide Notes** at the back of each title.

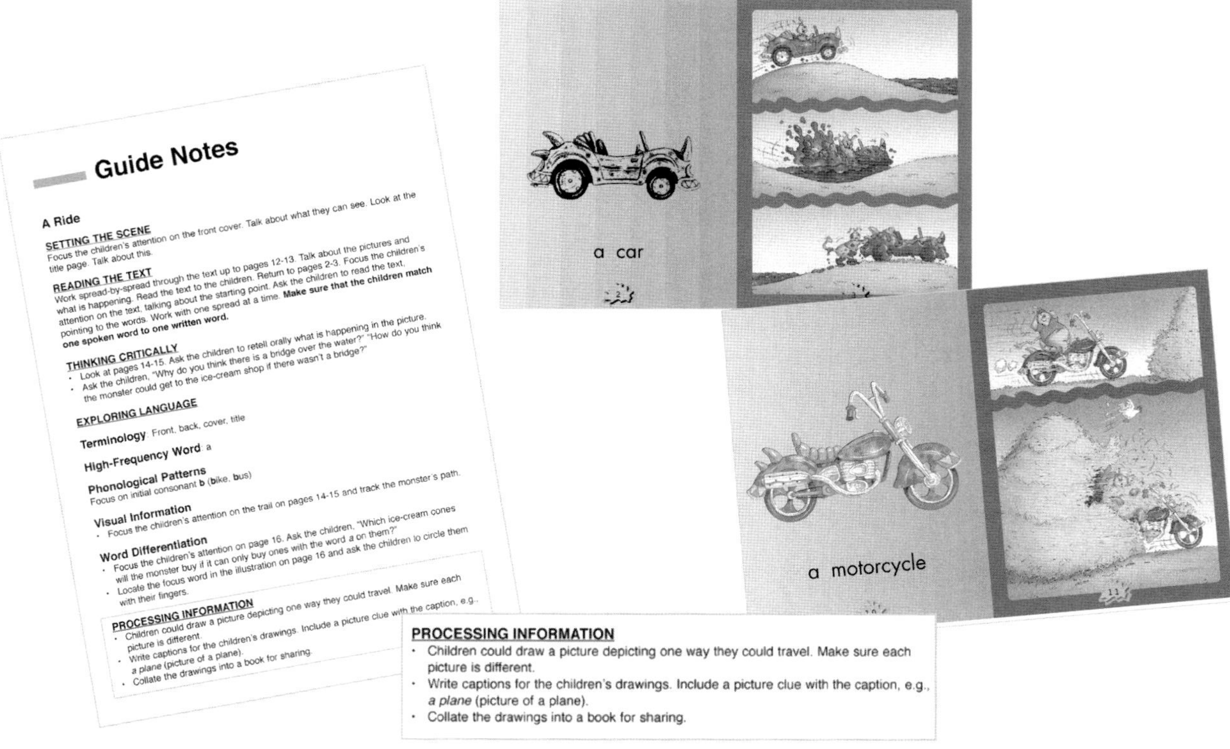

Guide Notes

A Ride

SETTING THE SCENE
Focus the children's attention on the front cover. Talk about what they can see. Look at the title page. Talk about this.

READING THE TEXT
Work spread-by-spread through the text up to pages 12-13. Talk about the pictures and what is happening. Read the text to the children. Return to pages 2-3. Focus the children's attention on the text, talking about the starting point. Ask the children to read the text, pointing to the words. Work with one spread at a time. **Make sure that the children match one spoken word to one written word.**

THINKING CRITICALLY
- Look at pages 14-15. Ask the children to retell orally what is happening in the picture.
- Ask the children, "Why do you think there is a bridge over the water?" "How do you think the monster could get to the ice-cream shop if there wasn't a bridge?"

EXPLORING LANGUAGE

Terminology: Front, back, cover, title

High-Frequency Word: a

Phonological Patterns
Focus on initial consonant **b** (**b**ike, **b**us)

Visual Information
- Focus the children's attention on the trail on pages 14-15 and track the monster's path.

Word Differentiation
- Focus the children's attention on page 16. Ask the children, "Which ice-cream cones will the monster buy if it can only buy ones with the word *a* on them?"
- Locate the focus word in the illustration on page 16 and ask the children to circle them with their fingers.

PROCESSING INFORMATION
- Children could draw a picture depicting one way they could travel. Make sure each picture is different.
- Write captions for the children's drawings. Include a picture clue with the caption, e.g., *a plane* (picture of a plane).
- Collate the drawings into a book for sharing.

PROCESSING INFORMATION
- Children could draw a picture depicting one way they could travel. Make sure each picture is different.
- Write captions for the children's drawings. Include a picture clue with the caption, e.g., *a plane* (picture of a plane).
- Collate the drawings into a book for sharing.

Achievement Objectives and Children's Targets

Learning is enhanced when there is a clear understanding of the learning goals.

Within this *Teacher's Resource Book*, objectives are provided in the strands of oral, written, and visual language for children functioning at the beginning stage of language development.

Achievement Objectives

The achievement objectives are the broad goals that will be achieved through the use of the *First Wave: Beginning Level* books. There are two types of objectives:

- language functions
- language processes

Language Functions

The language functions specify what the children are expected to be able to do. The following overview outlines the language functions that the *First Wave: Beginning Level* books support.

ORAL LANGUAGE – LISTENING AND SPEAKING

Functions: Interpersonal, Poetic, Transactional

Children are expected to be able to:

- converse and talk about meaning in text
- use texts to retell a story

WRITTEN LANGUAGE – READING

Functions: Personal Reading, Close Reading

Children are expected to be able to:

- respond to language and meaning in different texts, relating them to personal experience

VISUAL LANGUAGE

Functions: Presenting and Viewing

Children are expected to be able to:

- respond to meanings and ideas in the visual components of a text
- respond to meanings and ideas, identifying and describing simple verbal and visual features
- begin to record and present information

Language Processes

Language processes are crucial for language development. These processes are:

- thinking critically
- exploring language
- processing information

These processes encompass the three language strands. The *First Wave: Beginning Level* books support the following achievement objectives in the language processes.

Children are expected to be able to:

- identify and express meaning related to the texts, in response to questions drawing on personal experience
- identify some simple conventions of writing
- identify and retrieve some simple information from the texts
- understand that communication involves verbal and visual features
- view and use visual texts to gain and process information

Children's Targets

The children's targets are the specific objectives that will be achieved through the use of the *First Wave: Beginning Level* program at this initial stage of literacy.

Note: These targets can be focused on in a shared, guided, or independent reading program.

Oral Language

The children's targets are to:

- retell a story from a storyboard or visual
- talk about responses to a text
- express an opinion
- extend and enrich spoken vocabulary

Written Language

READING

The children's targets are to:

- match one spoken word to one written word
- retell a story in sequence from the visuals
- tell something about the characters
- identify the setting of the story
- interpret illustrations, and use illustrations to talk about and predict text
- demonstrate the front, back, and spine of a book
- have correct directional movement
- recognize some high-frequency words
- recognize some similarities in words
- make inferences from text and illustrations

WRITING

The children's targets are to:

- write some simple high-frequency words

Visual Language

The children's targets are to:

- look at simple visual information in the text and talk about the meaning

Phonological Patterns

The children's targets are to:

- see similarities in some words and match letters and words
- know the names of some letters
- know the sounds represented by some initial consonants

Reading Components

In order to meet the diverse needs of children, it is necessary to have a variety of approaches to the teaching of reading. These approaches are:

- reading **to** children
- reading **with** children
- reading **by** children

Within these approaches are the components of reading:

- Shared reading
- Guided reading
- Independent reading

Shared Reading

Refer to *Sails Teacher's Resource Book – Shared Reading* for details on this component.

Guided Reading

The *First Wave: Beginning Level* books used for guided reading at this stage focus on the foundational high-frequency words that children automatically need as beginning readers. They have a strong visual component that can be used for oral retelling, giving children the opportunity to predict and think critically. In each title, an interactive page provides opportunities for children to differentiate between simple high-frequency words. The achievement objectives and children's targets provided in this *Teacher's Resource Book* can be introduced and reinforced through the components of guided reading. Reinforcements are made for print conventions, high-frequency words, new vocabulary, phonological patterns, and visual information. (See following page.)

Leveling for Guided Reading

These books have been leveled at the very initial stage of guided reading. They begin with simple two-word captions or labels on one line, and progress to simple two-line sentences with a repeated structure. The high-frequency words are introduced and then reinforced throughout subsequent books.

Independent Reading

Independent reading needs to be encouraged at all stages of children's reading development. A wide variety of independent reading material must be provided in order for children to enjoy reading and practice their reading skills. In the *First Wave: Beginning Level*, guided reading texts will form part of the independent reading resource. These will now be familiar texts. Shared books that the children have been introduced to (*not* unseen texts) also become part of the independent reading resource.

Suggested Approach for Guided Reading at the Beginning Stage

For beginning readers, it is important to "form the foundation" of reading. This gives children an introduction to the storyline, vocabulary, and visual information in the book. The following format can be used:

Step One: Setting the Scene

- Focus the children's attention on the front cover. Talk about what they can see. Look at the title page. Talk about this.

Step Two: Reading the Text

- Work spread-by-spread through the text, up to pages 12-13. Talk about the pictures and what is happening. Read the text to the children. Return to pages 2-3. Focus the children's attention on the text, talking about the starting point. Ask the children to read the text, pointing to the words. Work with one spread at a time. Make sure the children match one spoken word to one written word.

Step Three: Thinking Critically

- Look at pages 14-15. Talk about these pages. Ask the children to retell orally what is happening in the pictures. Ask the children one or two critical-thinking questions: "What do you think . . .?" "What might happen if . . .?" Give the children the opportunity to relate the message of the visual story to their own experiences.

Step Four: Visual Information

- Focus the children's attention on the visual information on pages 14-15, or on its occurrence throughout the book, and discuss.

Step Five: Word Differentiation

- Look at page 16 and ask the children to identify the focus words. Look at the focus words in the illustration and ask the children to circle them with their fingers, or try to write them on a piece of paper.

Step Six: Phonological Patterns

- Focus on one initial consonant. Ask the children to circle the letter with their fingers or try to write the letter on a piece of paper.

Step Seven: Processing Information

- Use an idea in the text to stimulate a visual or written response that can be collated in a booklet for independent reading. (Note: Only one group per day should process information this way.)

Step Eight: Independent Reading

- Allow the children time to read the story independently. The book will continue to become part of each child's independent reading resource and can be practiced independently on a daily basis.

Key Features of the *First Wave: Beginning Level*

Vocabulary

It is important that children gradually accumulate a reading vocabulary of known words that they can recognize automatically and rapidly. Children need to acquire this vocabulary as much as possible through natural ways, in the context of reading and writing that has a purpose.

The *First Wave: Beginning Level* books provide children with an initial introduction to simple high-frequency words. Each high-frequency word is repeated in multiple texts, giving children the opportunity to practice the same word in a different context.

Print Information

As well as making sure that they are reading for meaning, teachers should check that children are actively learning about print information and characteristics of written text.

There are three sources of print information:

- print conventions
- phonological patterns
- visual information

Print Conventions

Print conventions help children find meaning. It is essential that print conventions are introduced and reinforced. While print conventions are not specifically focused on at this beginning stage, periods and capital letters are a first introduction to print conventions, and are the only ones present in the text at this level of guided reading.

Phonological Patterns

The *First Wave: Beginning Level* books provide an initial introduction to phonological knowledge. Children are introduced to some consonant letters and letter sounds. In the Guide Notes for each title, suggestions are made for focusing on initial consonants in the guided reading lesson.

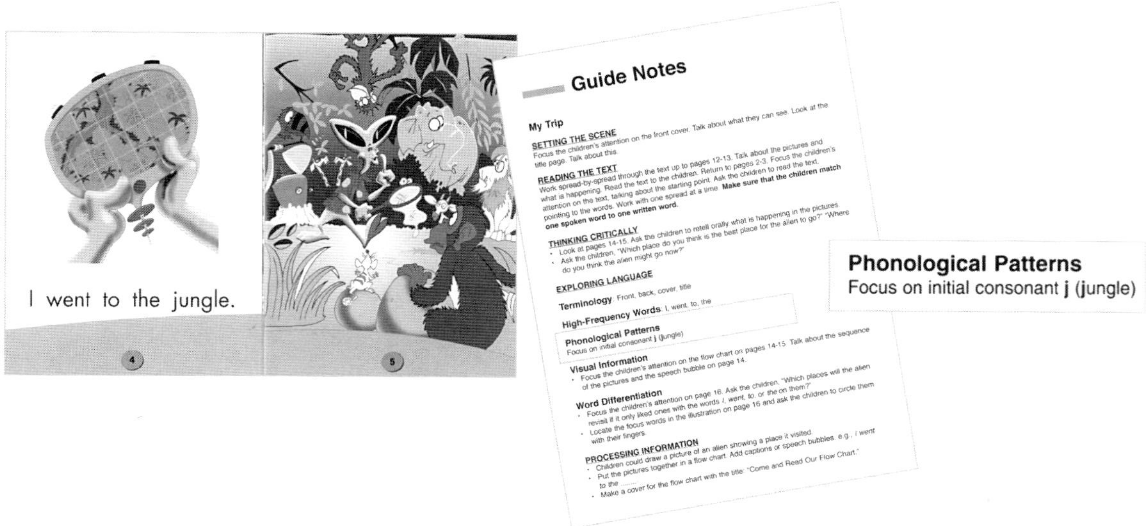

Visual Information

The *First Wave: Beginning Level* books introduce children to some simple examples of visual language, such as speech bubbles, storyboards, flow diagrams, trails, labels, symbols, maps, captions, and thought bubbles. The visual focus for each text is highlighted in the Guide Notes at the back of each book.

Guide Notes

The Guide Notes suggest ways in which children can be encouraged to think critically, explore language, interpret visual language, and process information.

Guide Notes

Dinner

SETTING THE SCENE
Focus the children's attention on the front cover. Talk about what they can see. Look at the title page. Talk about this.

READING THE TEXT
Work spread-by-spread through the text up to pages 12-13. Talk about the pictures and what is happening. Read the text to the children. Return to pages 2-3. Focus the children's attention on the text, talking about the starting point. Ask the children to read the text, pointing to the words. Work with one spread at a time. **Make sure that the children match one spoken word to one written word.**

THINKING CRITICALLY
- Look at pages 14-15. Ask the children to retell orally what is happening in the pictures.
- Ask the children, "Why do you think the farmer is using the wheelbarrow?" "Why do you think the monster looks happy?"

EXPLORING LANGUAGE

Terminology: Front, back, cover, title

High-Frequency Words: this, is, for, a

Phonological Patterns
Focus on initial consonant **d** (**d**og, **d**uck)

Visual Information
- Focus the children's attention on the storyboard on pages 14-15. Talk about the sequence of the pictures and the speech bubble on page 15.

Word Differentiation
- Focus the children's attention on page 16. Ask the children, "Which buckets of food will the monster choose if it can only choose ones with the words *this*, *is*, *for*, or *a* on them?"
- Locate the focus words in the illustration on page 16 and ask the children to circle them with their fingers.

PROCESSING INFORMATION
- Children could draw a picture of something a monster would like to eat.
- Write captions for the children's drawings, e.g., *This is for a monster.* Add labels to the pictures, e.g., *a banana*, *a cookie*.
- Collate the drawings into a book for sharing.

THINKING CRITICALLY
- Look at pages 14-15. Ask the children to retell orally what is happening in the pictures.
- Ask the children, "Why do you think the farmer is using the wheelbarrow?" "Why do you think the monster looks happy?"

Assessment and Evaluation

Assessment and evaluation are an integral part of the learning cycle. It is important to gain a clear picture of what each individual child can do and what the next steps in his or her learning should be. The following suggestions will provide data for assessment and evaluation purposes at this beginning stage of reading acquisition.

Observations

Observe children and gather information on:

- interest
- attitude
- oral language development
- phonological knowledge
- written language development

Samples of Work

Samples of writing and visual language are collected and analyzed. The children's knowledge of print conventions, phonological patterns, and visual information will emerge from this analysis.

Achievement Objectives and Target Checks

A regular check needs to be kept on the targets that children have achieved, so that new goals can continually be introduced. This *Teacher's Resource Book* provides checks in oral, written, and visual language at this beginning stage. (See pages 77–81.)

Assessment Tasks

Assessment Tasks have been provided for gathering further data to help teachers analyze what children know, and to give an insight into what further help may be needed. These Assessment Tasks cover the written and visual focus that has been introduced at this beginning stage. It is not necessary to use all the Assessment Tasks, but it is important to gain a clear insight into each child's developmental stage of learning.

Selected Assessment Tasks should be given to children after working through the appropriate books.

Independent Reinforcement Activities

Independent reinforcement activities have been included as a follow-up to the guided reading session. These activities provide valuable information about the individual child's developmental stage.

Guide Notes
First Wave: Beginning Level

Vocabulary

High-Frequency Words

a, the, my, I, can, like, am, here, this, is, look, at, see, went, we, in, to, put, on, and, for

Phonological Patterns

Initial Consonants

b, r, s, t, c, d, g, h, l, m, p, w, j, f

Visual Information

The following examples of visual language are focused on in the books:

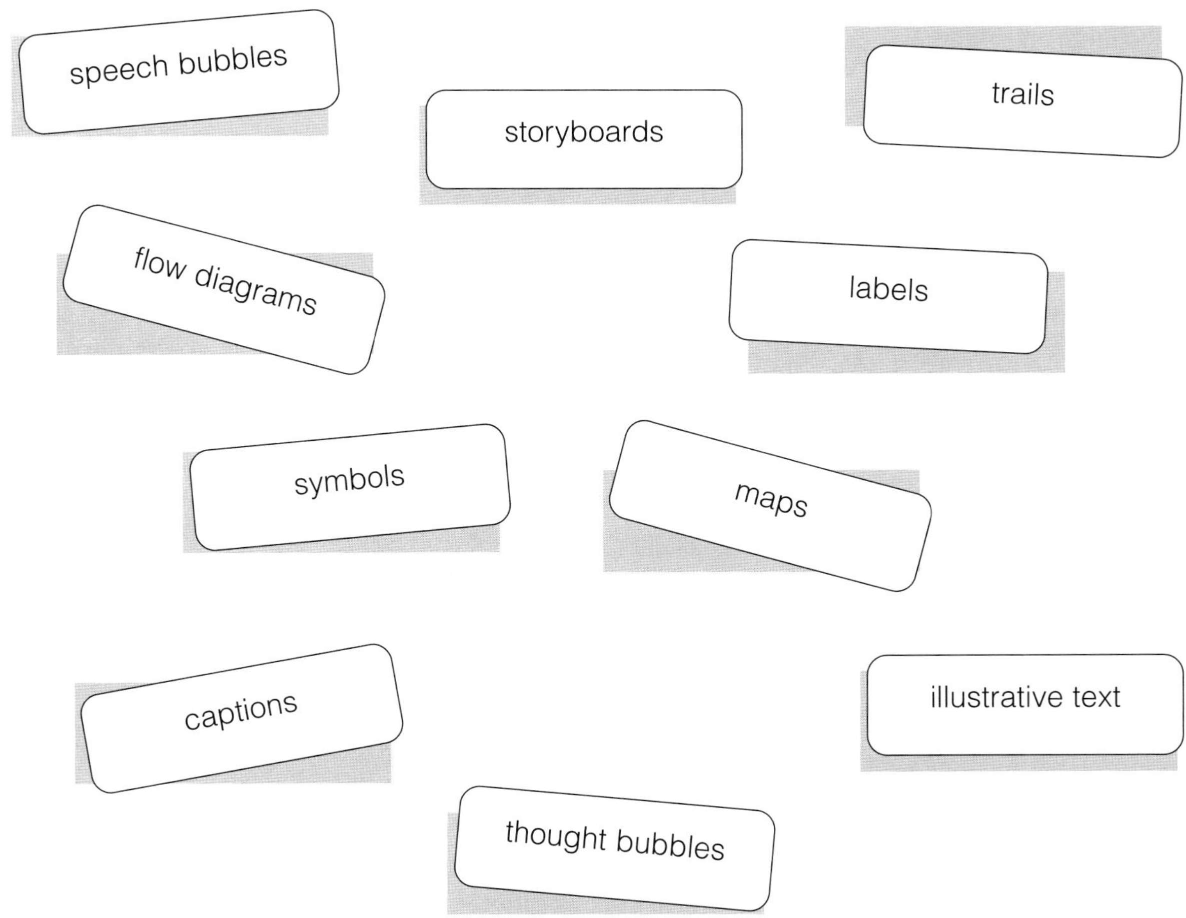

A Garden

Setting The Scene

Focus the children's attention on the front cover. Talk about what they can see. Look at the title page. Talk about this.

Reading The Text

Work spread-by-spread through the text up to pages 12-13. Talk about the pictures and what is happening. Read the text to the children. Return to pages 2-3. Focus the children's attention on the text, talking about the starting point. Ask the children to read the text, pointing to the words. Work with one spread at a time. **Make sure that the children match one spoken word to one written word.**

Thinking Critically

- Look at pages 14-15. Ask the children to retell orally what is happening in the pictures.
- Ask the children, "Why do you think the rabbit looks so fat?" "Where do you think the rabbit got all the food from?"

Exploring Language

Terminology: Front, back, cover, title

High-Frequency Word: a

Phonological Patterns

Focus on initial consonant **l** (**l**eaf)

Visual Information

- Focus the children's attention on the labels on pages 14-15. Talk about these.

Word Differentiation

- Focus the children's attention on page 16. Ask the children, "Which carrots will the rabbit eat if it can only eat ones with the word *a* on them?"
- Locate the focus word in the illustration on page 16 and ask the children to circle them with their fingers.

Processing Information

- Children could draw a picture of a garden.
- Write labels for the children's drawings, e.g., *a flower, a tree.*
- Collate the drawings into a book for sharing.

A Monster House

Setting The Scene

Focus the children's attention on the front cover. Talk about what they can see. Look at the title page. Talk about this.

Reading The Text

Work spread-by-spread through the text up to pages 12-13. Talk about the pictures and what is happening. Read the text to the children. Return to pages 2-3. Focus the children's attention on the text, talking about the starting point. Ask the children to read the text, pointing to the words. Work with one spread at a time. **Make sure that the children match one spoken word to one written word.**

Thinking Critically

- Look at pages 14-15. Ask the children to retell orally what is happening in the pictures.
- Ask the children, "Why do you think the monster's house fell down?" "What do you think the monster will do now?"

Exploring Language

Terminology: Front, back, cover, title

High-Frequency Word: a

Phonological Patterns

Focus on initial consonant **d** (**d**oor)

Visual Information

- Focus the children's attention on the labels on page 14. Talk about these.

Word Differentiation

- Focus the children's attention on page 16. Ask the children, "Which windows will the monster use in its house if it can only use ones with the word *a* on them?"
- Locate the focus word in the illustration on page 16 and ask the children to circle them with their fingers.

Processing Information

- Children could draw a picture of their house.
- Write labels for the children's drawings, e.g., *a door.*
- Collate the drawings into a book for sharing.

A Ride

Setting The Scene

Focus the children's attention on the front cover. Talk about what they can see. Look at the title page. Talk about this.

Reading The Text

Work spread-by-spread through the text up to pages 12-13. Talk about the pictures and what is happening. Read the text to the children. Return to pages 2-3. Focus the children's attention on the text, talking about the starting point. Ask the children to read the text, pointing to the words. Work with one spread at a time. **Make sure that the children match one spoken word to one written word.**

Thinking Critically

- Look at pages 14-15. Ask the children to retell orally what is happening in the picture.
- Ask the children, "Why do you think there is a bridge over the water?" "How do you think the monster could get to the ice-cream shop if there wasn't a bridge?"

Exploring Language

Terminology: Front, back, cover, title

High-Frequency Word: a

Phonological Patterns

Focus on initial consonant **b** (**b**ike, **b**us)

Visual Information

- Focus the children's attention on the trail on pages 14-15 and track the monster's path.

Word Differentiation

- Focus the children's attention on page 16. Ask the children, "Which ice-cream cones will the monster buy if it can only buy ones with the word *a* on them?"
- Locate the focus word in the illustration on page 16 and ask the children to circle them with their fingers.

Processing Information

- Children could draw a picture depicting one way they could travel. Make sure each picture is different.
- Write captions for the children's drawings. Include a picture clue with the caption, e.g., *a plane* (picture of a plane).
- Collate the drawings into a book for sharing.

A Home

Setting The Scene

Focus the children's attention on the front cover. Talk about what they can see. Look at the title page. Talk about this.

Reading The Text

Work spread-by-spread through the text up to pages 12-13. Talk about the pictures and what is happening. Read the text to the children. Return to pages 2-3. Focus the children's attention on the text, talking about the starting point. Ask the children to read the text, pointing to the words. Work with one spread at a time. **Make sure that the children match one spoken word to one written word.**

Thinking Critically

- Look at pages 14-15. Ask the children to retell orally what is happening in the picture.
- Ask the children, "How do you think the man feels about his house?" "What is different about your house and the man's house?"

Exploring Language

Terminology: Front, back, cover, title

High-Frequency Word: a

Phonological Patterns

Focus on initial consonant **t** (**t**able, **t**elevision)

Visual Information

- Focus the children's attention on the labels on pages 14-15. Talk about these.

Word Differentiation

- Focus the children's attention on page 16. Ask the children, "Which mirrors will the man use if he can only use ones with the word *a* on them?"
- Locate the focus word in the illustration on page 16 and ask the children to circle them with their fingers.

Processing Information

- Children could draw a floor plan of their house that shows where the furniture is placed.
- Write labels for the children's drawings, e.g., *a table.*
- Collate the drawings into a book for sharing.

The Jungle

Setting The Scene

Focus the children's attention on the front cover. Talk about what they can see. Look at the title page. Talk about this.

Reading The Text

Work spread-by-spread through the text up to pages 12-13. Talk about the pictures and what is happening. Read the text to the children. Return to pages 2-3. Focus the children's attention on the text, talking about the starting point. Ask the children to read the text, pointing to the words. Work with one spread at a time. **Make sure that the children match one spoken word to one written word.**

Thinking Critically

- Look at pages 14-15. Ask the children to retell orally what is happening in the picture.
- Ask the children, "Why do you think all the animals look happy?" "How do you know which things are presents?"

Exploring Language

Terminology: Front, back, cover, title

High-Frequency Word: the

Phonological Patterns

Focus on initial consonant **t** (**t**iger)

Visual Information

- Focus the children's attention on the labels on pages 14-15. Talk about these.

Word Differentiation

- Focus the children's attention on page 16. Ask the children, "Which presents will the crocodile open if it can only open ones with the word *the* on them?"
- Locate the focus word in the illustration on page 16 and ask the children to circle them with their fingers.

Processing Information

- Children could draw a picture of a party they have been to.
- Write labels for the children's drawings, e.g., *the cake*.
- Collate the drawings into a book for sharing.

The Farm

Setting The Scene

Focus the children's attention on the front cover. Talk about what they can see. Look at the title page. Talk about this.

Reading The Text

Work spread-by-spread through the text up to pages 12-13. Talk about the pictures and what is happening. Read the text to the children. Return to pages 2-3. Focus the children's attention on the text, talking about the starting point. Ask the children to read the text, pointing to the words. Work with one spread at a time. **Make sure that the children match one spoken word to one written word.**

Thinking Critically

- Look at pages 14-15. Ask the children to retell orally what is happening in the pictures.
- Ask the children, "Why do you think the farmer is chasing the animals?" "Why do you think the animals liked being in the house?"

Exploring Language

Terminology: Front, back, cover, title

High-Frequency Word: the

Phonological Patterns

Focus on initial consonant **h** (**h**en, **h**orse)

Visual Information

- Focus the children's attention on the labels on pages 14-15. Talk about these.

Word Differentiation

- Focus the children's attention on page 16. Ask the children, "Which animals will the farmer feed if he only has to feed the ones with the word *the* on them?"
- Locate the focus word in the illustration on page 16 and ask the children to circle them with their fingers.

Processing Information

- Children could draw a picture of a farm animal that they like. Paste the drawings onto a sheet of paper.
- Write labels for the children's drawings, e.g., *the horse*. Add a title such as, *The Farm*.
- Collate the drawings into a book for sharing.

The Day

Setting The Scene

Focus the children's attention on the front cover. Talk about what they can see. Look at the title page. Talk about this.

Reading The Text

Work spread-by-spread through the text up to pages 12-13. Talk about the pictures and what is happening. Read the text to the children. Return to pages 2-3. Focus the children's attention on the text, talking about the starting point. Ask the children to read the text, pointing to the words. Work with one spread at a time. **Make sure that the children match one spoken word to one written word.**

Thinking Critically

- Look at pages 14-15. Ask the children to retell orally what is happening in the pictures.
- Ask the children, "What do you think the owl will do in the daytime?" "What do you think the owl will do in the nighttime?"

Exploring Language

Terminology: Front, back, cover, title

High-Frequency Word: the

Phonological Patterns

Focus on initial consonant **m** (**m**oon)

Visual Information

- Focus the children's attention on the labels on pages 14-15 and the illustrative text on pages 7 and 13. Talk about these.

Word Differentiation

- Focus the children's attention on page 16. Ask the children, "Which stars will the moon choose if it can only choose ones with the word *the* on them?"
- Locate the focus word in the illustration on page 16 and ask the children to circle them with their fingers.

Processing Information

- Children could draw a nighttime picture or a daytime picture.
- Write labels for the children's drawings, e.g., *the moon.*
- Collate the drawings into a book for sharing.

The Monster's Clothes

Setting The Scene

Focus the children's attention on the front cover. Talk about what they can see. Look at the title page. Talk about this.

Reading The Text

Work spread-by-spread through the text up to pages 12-13. Talk about the pictures and what is happening. Read the text to the children. Return to pages 2-3. Focus the children's attention on the text, talking about the starting point. Ask the children to read the text, pointing to the words. Work with one spread at a time. **Make sure that the children match one spoken word to one written word.**

Thinking Critically

- Look at pages 14-15. Ask the children to retell orally what is happening in the pictures.
- Ask the children, "How do you think the monster feels about itself?" "Why do you think the monster put its shirt on before its cap?"

Exploring Language

Terminology: Front, back, cover, title

High-Frequency Word: the

Phonological Patterns
Focus on initial consonant **c** (**c**oat, **c**ap)

Visual Information
- Focus the children's attention on the labels on page 15. Talk about these.

Word Differentiation
- Focus the children's attention on page 16. Ask the children, "Which shirts will the monster buy if it can only buy ones with the word *the* on them?
- Locate the focus word in the illustration on page 16 and ask the children to circle them with their fingers.

Processing Information

- Children could draw a picture of themselves dressed to go out.
- Write labels for the children's drawings, e.g., *the shirt.*
- Collate the drawings into a book for sharing.

My Clothes

Setting The Scene

Focus the children's attention on the front cover. Talk about what they can see. Look at the title page. Talk about this.

Reading The Text

Work spread-by-spread through the text up to pages 12-13. Talk about the pictures and what is happening. Read the text to the children. Return to pages 2-3. Focus the children's attention on the text, talking about the starting point. Ask the children to read the text, pointing to the words. Work with one spread at a time. **Make sure that the children match one spoken word to one written word.**

Thinking Critically

- Look at pages 14-15. Ask the children to retell orally what is happening in the pictures.
- Ask the children, "Why do you think the little caterpillar is taking a sock?" "Look at the big caterpillar's face (page 15). Why do you think the big caterpillar is not happy?"

Exploring Language

Terminology: Front, back, cover, title

High-Frequency Word: my

Phonological Patterns

Focus on initial consonant **b** (**b**oots, **b**elt)

Visual Information

- Focus the children's attention on the speech bubble on page 15. Talk about this.

Word Differentiation

- Focus the children's attention on page 16. Ask the children, "Which socks will the big caterpillar wear if it can only wear ones with the word *my* on them?"
- Locate the focus word in the illustration on page 16 and ask the children to circle them with their fingers.

Processing Information

- Children could draw a picture of themselves dressed to go out.
- Write labels for the children's drawings, e.g., *my shirt.*
- Collate the drawings into a book for sharing.

My Family

Setting The Scene

Focus the children's attention on the front cover. Talk about what they can see. Look at the title page. Talk about this.

Reading The Text

Work spread-by-spread through the text up to pages 12-13. Talk about the pictures and what is happening. Read the text to the children. Return to pages 2-3. Focus the children's attention on the text, talking about the starting point. Ask the children to read the text, pointing to the words. Work with one spread at a time. **Make sure that the children match one spoken word to one written word.**

Thinking Critically

- Look at pages 14-15. Ask the children to retell orally what is happening in the pictures.
- Ask the children, "Why do you think the mouse looks so pleased with the cat?" "Why do you think the cat looks so pleased with the mouse?"

Exploring Language

Terminology: Front, back, cover, title

High-Frequency Word: my

Phonological Patterns

Focus on initial consonant **m** (**m**y, **m**other)

Visual Information

- Focus the children's attention on the speech bubble on page 15. Talk about this.

Word Differentiation

- Focus the children's attention on page 16. Ask the children, "Which cheeses will the mice have if they can only have ones with the word *my* on them?"
- Locate the focus word in the illustration on page 16 and ask the children to circle them with their fingers.

Processing Information

- Children could draw a picture of someone in their family.
- Write captions for the children's drawings, e.g., *my sister.*
- Collate the drawings into a book for sharing.

My Alien

Setting The Scene

Focus the children's attention on the front cover. Talk about what they can see. Look at the title page. Talk about this.

Reading The Text

Work spread-by-spread through the text up to pages 12-13. Talk about the pictures and what is happening. Read the text to the children. Return to pages 2-3. Focus the children's attention on the text, talking about the starting point. Ask the children to read the text, pointing to the words. Work with one spread at a time. **Make sure that the children match one spoken word to one written word.**

Thinking Critically

- Look at pages 14-15. Ask the children to retell orally what is happening in the pictures.
- Ask the children, "Where do you think the alien might be going?" "How can you tell it is a friendly alien?"

Exploring Language

Terminology: Front, back, cover, title

High-Frequency Word: my

Phonological Patterns

Focus on initial consonant **h** (**h**ead, **h**ands)

Visual Information

- Focus the children's attention on the speech bubble on page 15. Talk about this.

Word Differentiation

- Focus the children's attention on page 16. Ask the children, "Which stars will the alien visit if it can only visit ones with the word *my* on them?"
- Locate the focus word in the illustration on page 16 and ask the children to circle them with their fingers.

Processing Information

- Children could draw a picture of an alien.
- Write captions for the children's drawings, e.g., *my alien.*
- Collate the drawings into a book for sharing.

My Things

Setting The Scene

Focus the children's attention on the front cover. Talk about what they can see. Look at the title page. Talk about this.

Reading The Text

Work spread-by-spread through the text up to pages 12-13. Talk about the pictures and what is happening. Read the text to the children. Return to pages 2-3. Focus the children's attention on the text, talking about the starting point. Ask the children to read the text, pointing to the words. Work with one spread at a time. **Make sure that the children match one spoken word to one written word.**

Thinking Critically

- Look at pages 14-15. Ask the children to retell orally what is happening in the pictures.
- Ask the children, "Why do you think all the animals want to go for a ride?" "What do you think is dangerous about the ride?"

Exploring Language

Terminology: Front, back, cover, title

High-Frequency Word: my

Phonological Patterns

Focus on initial consonant **c** (**c**ar, **c**at)

Visual Information

- Focus the children's attention on the speech bubble on page 15. Talk about this.

Word Differentiation

- Focus the children's attention on page 16. Ask the children, "Which skateboards will the monster have if it can only have ones with the word *my* on them?"
- Locate the focus word in the illustration on page 16 and ask the children to circle them with their fingers.

Processing Information

- Children could draw a picture of a toy or a pet that they have.
- Write captions for the children's drawings, e.g., *my cat.*
- Collate the drawings into a book for sharing.

I Can

Setting The Scene

Focus the children's attention on the front cover. Talk about what they can see. Look at the title page. Talk about this.

Reading The Text

Work spread-by-spread through the text up to pages 12-13. Talk about the pictures and what is happening. Read the text to the children. Return to pages 2-3. Focus the children's attention on the text, talking about the starting point. Ask the children to read the text, pointing to the words. Work with one spread at a time. **Make sure that the children match one spoken word to one written word.**

Thinking Critically

- Look at pages 14-15. Ask the children to retell orally what is happening in the pictures.
- Ask the children, "Why do you think the mouse can't fly anymore?" "How do you think the bird will help the mouse?"

Exploring Language

Terminology: Front, back, cover, title

High-Frequency Words: I, can

Phonological Patterns

Focus on initial consonant **h** (**h**op)

Visual Information

- Focus the children's attention on the thought bubble on page 14 and the speech bubble on page 15. Talk about these.

Word Differentiation

- Focus the children's attention on page 16. Ask the children, "Which strawberries will the bird and mouse eat if they can only eat ones with the words *I* or *can* on them?"
- Locate the focus words in the illustration on page 16 and ask the children to circle them with their fingers.

Processing Information

- Children could draw a picture of something they can do.
- Write speech bubbles to add to the children's drawings, e.g., *I can* ____.
- Write captions for the children's drawings, e.g., *I am Jo*.
- Collate the drawings into a book for sharing.

I Can Laugh

Setting The Scene

Focus the children's attention on the front cover. Talk about what they can see. Look at the title page. Talk about this.

Reading The Text

Work spread-by-spread through the text up to pages 12-13. Talk about the pictures and what is happening. Read the text to the children. Return to pages 2-3. Focus the children's attention on the text, talking about the starting point. Ask the children to read the text, pointing to the words. Work with one spread at a time. **Make sure that the children match one spoken word to one written word.**

Thinking Critically

- Look at pages 14-15. Ask the children to retell orally what is happening in the pictures.
- Ask the children, "Why do you think the clown is laughing?" "Why do you think the clown is crying?"

Exploring Language

Terminology: Front, back, cover, title

High-Frequency Words: I, can

Phonological Patterns
Focus on initial consonant **l** (**l**augh)

Visual Information
- Focus the children's attention on the speech bubbles on pages 14-15. Talk about these.

Word Differentiation
- Focus the children's attention on page 16. Ask the children, "Which noses will the clown have if he can only have ones with the words *I* or *can* on them?"
- Locate the focus words in the illustration on page 16 and ask the children to circle them with their fingers.

Processing Information

- Children could draw a picture of a clown doing something.
- Write speech bubbles to add to the children's drawings, e.g., *I can* ____.
- Collate the drawings into a book for sharing.

The Animals

Setting The Scene

Focus the children's attention on the front cover. Talk about what they can see. Look at the title page. Talk about this.

Reading The Text

Work spread-by-spread through the text up to pages 12-13. Talk about the pictures and what is happening. Read the text to the children. Return to pages 2-3. Focus the children's attention on the text, talking about the starting point. Ask the children to read the text, pointing to the words. Work with one spread at a time. **Make sure that the children match one spoken word to one written word.**

Thinking Critically

- Look at pages 14-15. Ask the children to retell orally what is happening in the picture.
- Ask the children, "Why do you think the burglar is frightened?" "What do you think the burglar might do now?"

Exploring Language

Terminology: Front, back, cover, title

High-Frequency Words: I, can

Phonological Patterns

Focus on initial consonant **m** (**m**eow, **m**oo)

Visual Information

- Focus the children's attention on the illustrative text throughout the book and the speech bubble on page 15. Talk about these.

Word Differentiation

- Focus the children's attention on page 16. Ask the children, "Which eggs belong to the duck if hers are the ones with the words *I* or *can* on them?"
- Locate the focus words in the illustration on page 16 and ask the children to circle them with their fingers.

Processing Information

- Children could draw a picture of an animal.
- Write speech bubbles to add to the children's drawings that show the noise the animal makes, e.g., *I can quack*.
- Collate the drawings into a book for sharing.

I Can Swim

Setting The Scene

Focus the children's attention on the front cover. Talk about what they can see. Look at the title page. Talk about this.

Reading The Text

Work spread-by-spread through the text up to pages 12-13. Talk about the pictures and what is happening. Read the text to the children. Return to pages 2-3. Focus the children's attention on the text, talking about the starting point. Ask the children to read the text, pointing to the words. Work with one spread at a time. **Make sure that the children match one spoken word to one written word.**

Thinking Critically

- Look at pages 14-15. Ask the children to retell orally what is happening in the picture.
- Ask the children, "Why do you think the elephant is squirting the warthog?" "How do you know the other animals are happy with the elephant?"

Exploring Language

Terminology: Front, back, cover, title

High-Frequency Words: I, can

Phonological Patterns

Focus on initial consonant **j** (**j**ump)

Visual Information

- Focus the children's attention on the speech bubble on page 14. Talk about this.

Word Differentiation

- Focus the children's attention on page 16. Ask the children, "Which mud puddles will the warthog use if it can only use ones with the words *I* or *can* on them?"
- Locate the focus words in the illustration on page 16 and ask the children to circle them with their fingers.

Processing Information

- Children could draw a picture of an animal doing something.
- Write speech bubbles to add to the children's drawings, e.g., *I can climb.*
- Collate the drawings into a book for sharing.

I Like Riding

Setting The Scene

Focus the children's attention on the front cover. Talk about what they can see. Look at the title page. Talk about this.

Reading The Text

Work spread-by-spread through the text up to pages 12-13. Talk about the pictures and what is happening. Read the text to the children. Return to pages 2-3. Focus the children's attention on the text, talking about the starting point. Ask the children to read the text, pointing to the words. Work with one spread at a time. **Make sure that the children match one spoken word to one written word.**

Thinking Critically

- Look at pages 14-15. Ask the children to retell orally what is happening in the pictures.
- Ask the children, "Why do you think the balloon broke?" "Why do you think the mouse is walking away from the lion?"

Exploring Language

Terminology: Front, back, cover, title

High-Frequency Words: I, like

Phonological Patterns

Focus on initial consonant **r** (**r**iding)

Visual Information

- Focus the children's attention on the speech bubbles on page 15. Talk about these.

Word Differentiation

- Focus the children's attention on page 16. Ask the children, "Which balloons will the mouse have if it can only have ones with the words *I* or *like* on them?"
- Locate the focus words in the illustration on page 16 and ask the children to circle them with their fingers.

Processing Information

- Children could draw a picture of themselves doing something they like.
- Write speech bubbles to add to the children's drawings, e.g., *I like swimming.*
- Collate the drawings into a book for sharing.

I Like Hats

Setting The Scene

Focus the children's attention on the front cover. Talk about what they can see. Look at the title page. Talk about this.

Reading The Text

Work spread-by-spread through the text up to pages 12-13. Talk about the pictures and what is happening. Read the text to the children. Return to pages 2-3. Focus the children's attention on the text, talking about the starting point. Ask the children to read the text, pointing to the words. Work with one spread at a time. **Make sure that the children match one spoken word to one written word.**

Thinking Critically

- Look at pages 14-15. Ask the children to retell orally what is happening in the pictures.
- Ask the children, "Why do you think the clown is not very happy?" "Why do you think the clown has a big check mark above the word hats?"

Exploring Language

Terminology: Front, back, cover, title

High-Frequency Words: I, like

Phonological Patterns

Focus on initial consonant **t** (**t**ies)

Visual Information

- Focus the children's attention on the speech bubble on page 15. Talk about this.

Word Differentiation

- Focus the children's attention on page 16. Ask the children, "Which hats will the clown buy if he can only buy ones with the words *I* or *like* on them?"
- Locate the focus words in the illustration on page 16 and ask the children to circle them with their fingers.

Processing Information

- Children could draw a picture of themselves as a clown. Ask them to choose one thing they would like to wear if they were clowns and put this in their picture.
- Write captions for the children's drawings, e.g., *I like shoes.*
- Collate the drawings into a book for sharing.

I Like Red

Setting The Scene

Focus the children's attention on the front cover. Talk about what they can see. Look at the title page. Talk about this.

Reading The Text

Work spread-by-spread through the text up to pages 12-13. Talk about the pictures and what is happening. Read the text to the children. Return to pages 2-3. Focus the children's attention on the text, talking about the starting point. Ask the children to read the text, pointing to the words. Work with one spread at a time. **Make sure that the children match one spoken word to one written word.**

Thinking Critically

- Look at pages 14-15. Ask the children to retell orally what is happening in the pictures.
- Ask the children, "Why do you think the boy is shooing away the birds?" "Why do you think he is letting the red birds sit on him?"

Exploring Language

Terminology: Front, back, cover, title

High-Frequency Words: I, like

Phonological Patterns

Focus on initial consonant **r** (**r**ed)

Visual Information

- Focus the children's attention on the speech bubble on page 15. Talk about this.

Word Differentiation

- Focus the children's attention on page 16. Ask the children, "Which trees will the birds fly to if they can only fly to ones with the words *I* or *like* on them?"
- Locate the focus words in the illustration on page 16 and ask the children to circle them with their fingers.

Processing Information

- Children could draw a picture of their favorite color birds.
- Write captions for the children's drawings, e.g., *I like yellow birds.*
- Collate the drawings into a book for sharing.

I Like Elephants

Setting The Scene

Focus the children's attention on the front cover. Talk about what they can see. Look at the title page. Talk about this.

Reading The Text

Work spread-by-spread through the text up to pages 12-13. Talk about the pictures and what is happening. Read the text to the children. Return to pages 2-3. Focus the children's attention on the text, talking about the starting point. Ask the children to read the text, pointing to the words. Work with one spread at a time. **Make sure that the children match one spoken word to one written word.**

Thinking Critically

- Look at pages 14-15. Ask the children to retell orally what is happening in the pictures.
- Ask the children, "Why do you think the monkeys are running away from the boy?" "How can you tell the elephants like the boy?"

Exploring Language

Terminology: Front, back, cover, title

High-Frequency Words: I, like

Phonological Patterns

Focus on initial consonant **b** (**b**irds, **b**ears, **b**ees)

Visual Information

- Focus the children's attention on the speech bubbles on pages 14-15. Talk about these.

Word Differentiation

- Focus the children's attention on page 16. Ask the children, "Which apples will the elephant have if it can only have ones with the words *I* or *like* on them?"
- Locate the focus words in the illustration on page 16 and ask the children to circle them with their fingers.

Processing Information

- Children could draw a picture of themselves. They could use magazines to find a picture of something that they like, and cut it out to paste onto their drawing.
- Write speech bubbles to add to the children's drawings, e.g., *I like* ____.
- Collate the pictures into a book for sharing.

I Am Jumping

Setting The Scene

Focus the children's attention on the front cover. Talk about what they can see. Look at the title page. Talk about this.

Reading The Text

Work spread-by-spread through the text up to pages 12-13. Talk about the pictures and what is happening. Read the text to the children. Return to pages 2-3. Focus the children's attention on the text, talking about the starting point. Ask the children to read the text, pointing to the words. Work with one spread at a time. **Make sure that the children match one spoken word to one written word.**

Thinking Critically

- Look at pages 14-15. Ask the children to retell orally what is happening in the pictures.
- Ask the children, "Why do you think things keep falling off the clown?" "What do you think the clown could do next?"

Exploring Language

Terminology: Front, back, cover, title

High-Frequency Words: I, am

Phonological Patterns

Focus on initial consonant **j** (**j**umping)

Visual Information

- Focus the children's attention on the flow chart on pages 14-15. Talk about the sequence of the pictures and the speech bubble on page 14.

Word Differentiation

- Focus the children's attention on page 16. Ask the children, "Which things will the clown put on if he can only put on things with the words *I* or *am* on them?"
- Locate the focus words in the illustration on page 16 and ask the children to circle them with their fingers.

Processing Information

- Children could draw a picture of a clown doing something.
- Write captions for the children's drawings, e.g., *I am running.*
- Collate the drawings into a book for sharing.

Monkeys

Setting The Scene

Focus the children's attention on the front cover. Talk about what they can see. Look at the title page. Talk about this.

Reading The Text

Work spread-by-spread through the text up to pages 12-13. Talk about the pictures and what is happening. Read the text to the children. Return to pages 2-3. Focus the children's attention on the text, talking about the starting point. Ask the children to read the text, pointing to the words. Work with one spread at a time. **Make sure that the children match one spoken word to one written word.**

Thinking Critically

- Look at pages 14-15. Ask the children to retell orally what is happening in the pictures.
- Ask the children, "Why do you think the monkey in the tree is clapping its hands?" "What do you think might happen to the monkey sliding down the tree?"

Exploring Language

Terminology: Front, back, cover, title

High-Frequency Words: I, am

Phonological Patterns

Focus on initial consonant **r** (**r**unning)

Visual Information

- Focus the children's attention on the thought bubbles on page 14 and the speech bubble on page 15. Talk about these.

Word Differentiation

- Focus the children's attention on page 16. Ask the children, "Which bananas will the monkeys eat if they can only eat ones with the words *I* or *am* on them?"
- Locate the focus words in the illustration on page 16 and ask the children to circle them with their fingers.

Processing Information

- Children could draw a picture of themselves either laughing, crying, sleeping, or eating.
- Write speech bubbles to add to the children's drawings, e.g., *I am laughing.*
- Write captions for the children's drawings, e.g., *I am Mark.*
- Collate the drawings into a book for sharing.

Sailors

Setting The Scene

Focus the children's attention on the front cover. Talk about what they can see. Look at the title page. Talk about this.

Reading The Text

Work spread-by-spread through the text up to pages 12-13. Talk about the pictures and what is happening. Read the text to the children. Return to pages 2-3. Focus the children's attention on the text, talking about the starting point. Ask the children to read the text, pointing to the words. Work with one spread at a time. **Make sure that the children match one spoken word to one written word.**

Thinking Critically

- Look at pages 14-15. Ask the children to retell orally what is happening in the pictures.
- Ask the children, "Why do you think the sailor is sleepy?" "Why do you think the other sailors wanted to wake him up?"

Exploring Language

Terminology: Front, back, cover, title

High-Frequency Words: I, am

Phonological Patterns

Focus on initial consonant **w** (**w**ashing)

Visual Information

- Focus the children's attention on the speech bubbles and the *zzz* in the illustration on page 14. Talk about these.

Word Differentiation

- Focus the children's attention on page 16. Ask the children, "Which fish will the sailor feed to the birds if he can only use ones with the words *I* or *am* on them?"
- Locate the focus words in the illustration on page 16 and ask the children to circle them with their fingers.

Processing Information

- Children can draw a picture of themselves doing jobs they would like to do if they were sailors.
- Write captions for the children's drawings, e.g., *I am cooking.*
- Collate the drawings into a book for sharing.

I Am Working

Setting The Scene

Focus the children's attention on the front cover. Talk about what they can see. Look at the title page. Talk about this.

Reading The Text

Work spread-by-spread through the text up to pages 12-13. Talk about the pictures and what is happening. Read the text to the children. Return to pages 2-3. Focus the children's attention on the text, talking about the starting point. Ask the children to read the text, pointing to the words. Work with one spread at a time. **Make sure that the children match one spoken word to one written word.**

Thinking Critically

- Look at pages 14-15. Ask the children to retell orally what is happening in the pictures.
- Ask the children, "Why do you think the monster might have knocked down the jars?" "Why do you think the monster threw the cookies to the birds?"

Exploring Language

Terminology: Front, back, cover, title

High-Frequency Words: I, am

Phonological Patterns

Focus on initial consonant **w** (**w**ashing)

Visual Information

- Focus the children's attention on the speech bubbles and illustrative text on pages 14-15. Talk about these.

Word Differentiation

- Focus the children's attention on page 16. Ask the children, "Which paint cans will the monster buy if it can only buy ones with the words *I* or *am* on them?"
- Locate the focus words in the illustration on page 16 and ask the children to circle them with their fingers.

Processing Information

- Children could draw a picture of a monster doing something.
- Write speech bubbles to add to the children's drawings, e.g., *I am* ____.
- Write captions for the children's drawings, e.g., *I am Fred.*
- Collate the drawings into a book for sharing.

The Goats

Setting The Scene

Focus the children's attention on the front cover. Talk about what they can see. Look at the title page. Talk about this.

Reading The Text

Work spread-by-spread through the text up to pages 12-13. Talk about the pictures and what is happening. Read the text to the children. Return to pages 2-3. Focus the children's attention on the text, talking about the starting point. Ask the children to read the text, pointing to the words. Work with one spread at a time. **Make sure that the children match one spoken word to one written word.**

Thinking Critically

- Look at pages 14-15. Ask the children to retell orally what is happening in the pictures.
- Ask the children, "Why do you think the goats want to go over the bridge?" "Why do you think the monster doesn't want the goats to go over the bridge?"

Exploring Language

Terminology: Front, back, cover, title

High-Frequency Words: I, am, a

Phonological Patterns

Focus on initial consonant **g** (**g**oat)

Visual Information

- Focus the children's attention on the speech bubbles on page 14. Talk about these.

Word Differentiation

- Focus the children's attention on page 16. Ask the children, "Which flowers will the goats have if they can only have ones with the words *I, am,* or *a* on them?"
- Locate the focus words in the illustration on page 16 and ask the children to circle them with their fingers.

Processing Information

- Children could draw a picture of a monster.
- Write speech bubbles to add to the children's drawings, e.g., *I am a monster.*
- Collate the drawings into a book for sharing.

The Family

Setting The Scene

Focus the children's attention on the front cover. Talk about what they can see. Look at the title page. Talk about this.

Reading The Text

Work spread-by-spread through the text up to pages 12-13. Talk about the pictures and what is happening. Read the text to the children. Return to pages 2-3. Focus the children's attention on the text, talking about the starting point. Ask the children to read the text, pointing to the words. Work with one spread at a time. **Make sure that the children match one spoken word to one written word.**

Thinking Critically

- Look at pages 14-15. Ask the children to retell orally what is happening in the pictures.
- Ask the children, "Why do you think the cat is chasing the robot?" "What do you think will happen to the robot?"

Exploring Language

Terminology: Front, back, cover, title

High-Frequency Words: I, am, a

Phonological Patterns

Focus on initial consonant **c** (**c**at)

Visual Information

- Focus the children's attention on the thought bubble on page 13 and the speech bubble on page 15. Talk about these.

Word Differentiation

- Focus the children's attention on page 16. Ask the children, "Which stars will the family visit if they can only visit ones with the words *I, am,* or *a* on them?"
- Locate the focus words in the illustration on page 16 and ask the children to circle them with their fingers.

Processing Information

- Children could draw a picture of someone in their family.
- Write speech bubbles to add to the children's drawings, e.g., *I am a* ____.
- Collate the drawings into a book for sharing.

I Am a Painter

Setting The Scene

Focus the children's attention on the front cover. Talk about what they can see. Look at the title page. Talk about this.

Reading The Text

Work spread-by-spread through the text up to pages 12-13. Talk about the pictures and what is happening. Read the text to the children. Return to pages 2-3. Focus the children's attention on the text, talking about the starting point. Ask the children to read the text, pointing to the words. Work with one spread at a time. **Make sure that the children match one spoken word to one written word.**

Thinking Critically

- Look at pages 14-15. Ask the children to retell orally what is happening in the pictures.
- Ask the children, "Why do you think the truck driver crashed into the light?" "What do you think the policeman is writing in his notebook?"

Exploring Language

Terminology: Front, back, cover, title

High-Frequency Words: I, am, a

Phonological Patterns

Focus on initial consonant **p** (**p**ainter, **p**oliceman)

Visual Information

- Focus the children's attention on the speech bubble on page 15. Talk about this.

Word Differentiation

- Focus the children's attention on page 16. Ask the children, "Which paint cans will the painter buy if he can only buy ones with the words *I, am,* or *a* on them?"
- Locate the focus words in the illustration on page 16 and ask the children to circle them with their fingers.

Processing Information

- Children could draw a picture of themselves doing a job they think they would like.
- Write speech bubbles to add to the children's drawings, e.g., *I am a* ____.
- Collate the drawings into a book for sharing.

I Am a Bee

Setting the Scene

Focus the children's attention on the front cover. Talk about what they can see. Look at the title page. Talk about this.

Reading the Text

Work spread-by-spread through the text up to pages 12-13. Talk about the pictures and what is happening. Read the text to the children. Return to pages 2-3. Focus the children's attention on the text, talking about the starting point. Ask the children to read the text, pointing to the words. Work with one spread at a time. **Make sure that the children match one spoken word to one written word.**

Thinking Critically

- Look at pages 14-15. Ask the children to retell orally what is happening in the pictures.
- Ask the children, "Why do you think the animals are chasing each other?" "Why do you think all the animals are running away?"

Exploring Language

Terminology: Front, back, cover, title

High-Frequency Words: I, am, a

Phonological Patterns
Focus on initial consonant **g** (**g**oat)

Visual Information
- Focus the children's attention on the speech bubble on page 15. Talk about this.

Word Differentiation
- Focus the children's attention on page 16. Ask the children, "Which flowers will the bee use if it can only use ones with the words *I, am,* or *a* on them?"
- Locate the focus words in the illustration on page 16 and ask the children to circle them with their fingers.

Processing Information

- Children could draw a picture of an animal.
- Write captions for the children's drawings. Include a picture clue with the caption, e.g., *I am a cat* (picture of a cat).
- Collate the drawings into a book for sharing.

Here Is a Bird

Setting The Scene

Focus the children's attention on the front cover. Talk about what they can see. Look at the title page. Talk about this.

Reading The Text

Work spread-by-spread through the text up to pages 12-13. Talk about the pictures and what is happening. Read the text to the children. Return to pages 2-3. Focus the children's attention on the text, talking about the starting point. Ask the children to read the text, pointing to the words. Work with one spread at a time. **Make sure that the children match one spoken word to one written word.**

Thinking Critically

- Look at pages 14-15. Ask the children to retell orally what is happening in the pictures.
- Ask the children, "Why do you think the man looked unhappy when the snake came out of the hat?" "Why do you think the bird might have taken the man's wand?"

Exploring Language

Terminology: Front, back, cover, title

High-Frequency Words: here, is, a

Phonological Patterns

Focus on initial consonant **b** (**b**all, **b**ook, **b**alloon, **b**anana, **b**ird)

Visual Information

- Focus the children's attention on the speech bubbles on page 14. Talk about these.

Word Differentiation

- Focus the children's attention on page 16. Ask the children, "Which balloons will the man use if he can only use ones with the words *here, is,* or *a* on them?"
- Locate the focus words in the illustration on page 16 and ask the children to circle them with their fingers.

Processing Information

- Children could draw a picture of themselves with a hat and a wand. They can draw something coming out of their hat, e.g., a cat, a mouse, etc.
- Write captions for the children's drawings. Include a picture clue with the caption, e.g., *Here is a cat* (picture of a cat).
- Collate the drawings into a book for sharing.

The Show

Setting The Scene

Focus the children's attention on the front cover. Talk about what they can see. Look at the title page. Talk about this.

Reading The Text

Work spread-by-spread through the text up to pages 12-13. Talk about the pictures and what is happening. Read the text to the children. Return to pages 2-3. Focus the children's attention on the text, talking about the starting point. Ask the children to read the text, pointing to the words. Work with one spread at a time. **Make sure that the children match one spoken word to one written word.**

Thinking Critically

- Look at pages 14-15. Ask the children to retell orally what is happening in the pictures.
- Ask the children, "What do you think the lion is giving to the snake and the monkey?" "Why do you think the bird is flying away with the ribbon?"

Exploring Language

Terminology: Front, back, cover, title

High-Frequency Words: here, is, a

Phonological Patterns
Focus on initial consonant **m** (**m**onkey)

Visual Information
- Focus the children's attention on the speech bubble on page 15. Talk about this.

Word Differentiation
- Focus the children's attention on page 16. Ask the children, "Which ribbons will the animals have if they can only have ones with the words *here, is,* or *a* on them?"
- Locate the focus words in the illustration on page 16 and ask the children to circle them with their fingers.

Processing Information

- Children could draw a picture of a jungle animal.
- Write captions for the children's drawings, e.g., *Here is a lion.*
- Collate the drawings into a book for sharing.

The Party

Setting The Scene

Focus the children's attention on the front cover. Talk about what they can see. Look at the title page. Talk about this.

Reading The Text

Work spread-by-spread through the text up to pages 12-13. Talk about the pictures and what is happening. Read the text to the children. Return to pages 2-3. Focus the children's attention on the text, talking about the starting point. Ask the children to read the text, pointing to the words. Work with one spread at a time. **Make sure that the children match one spoken word to one written word.**

Thinking Critically

- Look at pages 14-15. Ask the children to retell orally what is happening in the picture.
- Ask the children, "Why do you think the icing is flying off the cake?" "What do you think might happen if the monster kept on blowing?"

Exploring Language

Terminology: Front, back, cover, title

High-Frequency Words: here, is, the

Phonological Patterns

Focus on initial consonant **p** (**p**izza, **p**ie)

Visual Information

- Focus the children's attention on the caption on page 14 and the labels on pages 14-15. Talk about these.

Word Differentiation

- Focus the children's attention on page 16. Ask the children, "Which boxes will the monster open if it can only open ones with the words *here, is,* or *the* on them?"
- Locate the focus words in the illustration on page 16 and ask the children to circle them with their fingers.

Processing Information

- Children could find something in a magazine that could be the present inside the box for the monster. Cut out the pictures and paste them onto a sheet of paper.
- Write captions for the selected magazine pictures, e.g., *Here is the shoe.*
- Collate the pictures into a book for sharing.

The Water Park

Setting The Scene

Focus the children's attention on the front cover. Talk about what they can see. Look at the title page. Talk about this.

Reading The Text

Work spread-by-spread through the text up to pages 12-13. Talk about the pictures and what is happening. Read the text to the children. Return to pages 2-3. Focus the children's attention on the text, talking about the starting point. Ask the children to read the text, pointing to the words. Work with one spread at a time. **Make sure that the children match one spoken word to one written word.**

Thinking Critically

- Look at pages 14-15. Ask the children to retell orally what is happening in the pictures.
- Ask the children, "Why do you think the penguin shouldn't go into the other pools?" "What do you think the diver is going to do with the penguin?"

Exploring Language

Terminology: Front, back, cover, title

High-Frequency Words: here, is, the

Phonological Patterns
Focus on initial consonant **d** (**d**olphin, **d**iver)

Visual Information
- Focus the children's attention on the symbols and signs on pages 14-15. Talk about these and their messages.

Word Differentiation
- Focus the children's attention on page 16. Ask the children, "If the penguins with the words *here, is,* and *the* are the hungriest penguins, which ones should have food first?"
- Locate the focus words in the illustration on page 16 and ask the children to circle them with their fingers.

Processing Information

- Children could draw a picture of an animal that would be found in a water park like the one here.
- Write signs for the children's drawings, e.g., *Here is the whale.*
- Collate the drawings into a book for sharing.

In the Garden

Setting The Scene

Focus the children's attention on the front cover. Talk about what they can see. Look at the title page. Talk about this.

Reading The Text

Work spread-by-spread through the text up to pages 12-13. Talk about the pictures and what is happening. Read the text to the children. Return to pages 2-3. Focus the children's attention on the text, talking about the starting point. Ask the children to read the text, pointing to the words. Work with one spread at a time. **Make sure that the children match one spoken word to one written word.**

Thinking Critically

- Look at pages 14-15. Ask the children to retell orally what is happening in the picture.
- Ask the children, "Why do you think the monster is running?" "Where do you think the monster might be running to?"

Exploring Language

Terminology: Front, back, cover, title

High-Frequency Words: this, is, a

Phonological Patterns

Focus on initial consonant **b** (**b**eetle, **b**ee, **b**utterfly)

Visual Information

- Focus the children's attention on the thought bubble on page 15. Talk about this.

Word Differentiation

- Focus the children's attention on page 16. Ask the children, "Which screens will the monster work on if it can only work on ones with the words *this, is,* or *a* on them?"
- Locate the focus words in the illustration on page 16 and ask the children to circle them with their fingers.

Processing Information

- Children could draw a picture of a monster and an insect in a different garden.
- Write captions for the children's drawings, e.g., *This is a* ____.
- Collate the drawings into a book for sharing.

A Shoe

Setting The Scene

Focus the children's attention on the front cover. Talk about what they can see. Look at the title page. Talk about this.

Reading The Text

Work spread-by-spread through the text up to pages 12-13. Talk about the pictures and what is happening. Read the text to the children. Return to pages 2-3. Focus the children's attention on the text, talking about the starting point. Ask the children to read the text, pointing to the words. Work with one spread at a time. **Make sure that the children match one spoken word to one written word.**

Thinking Critically

- Look at pages 14-15. Ask the children to retell orally what is happening in the pictures.
- Ask the children, "Why do you think the man put his foot in the bucket?" "Where do you think the man found his other shoe?"

Exploring Language

Terminology: Front, back, cover, title

High-Frequency Words: this, is, a

Phonological Patterns

Focus on initial consonant **s** (**s**ock)

Visual Information

- Focus the children's attention on the storyboard on pages 14-15. Talk about the sequence of the pictures and the captions on page 14.

Word Differentiation

- Focus the children's attention on page 16. Ask the children, "Which hats will the man buy if he can only buy ones with the words *this, is,* or *a* on them?"
- Locate the focus words in the illustration on page 16 and ask the children to circle them with their fingers.

Processing Information

- Children could draw a picture of themselves putting something on their foot.
- Write captions for the children's drawings, e.g., *This is a ____.*
- Collate the drawings into a book for sharing.

The Hole

Setting The Scene

Focus the children's attention on the front cover. Talk about what they can see. Look at the title page. Talk about this.

Reading The Text

Work spread-by-spread through the text up to pages 12-13. Talk about the pictures and what is happening. Read the text to the children. Return to pages 2-3. Focus the children's attention on the text, talking about the starting point. Ask the children to read the text, pointing to the words. Work with one spread at a time. **Make sure that the children match one spoken word to one written word.**

Thinking Critically

- Look at pages 14-15. Ask the children to retell orally what is happening in the picture.
- Ask the children, "Why do you think these animals are having a party underground?" "What do you think it would be like underground?"

Exploring Language

Terminology: Front, back, cover, title

High-Frequency Words: this, is, the

Phonological Patterns
Focus on initial consonant **r** (**r**at, **r**abbit)

Visual Information
- Focus the children's attention on the map on pages 14-15 depicting the underground homes. Talk about the map's information and the caption on page 15.

Word Differentiation
- Focus the children's attention on page 16. Ask the children: "Which party things will the animals choose if they can only choose ones with the words *this, is,* or *the* on them?"
- Locate the focus words in the illustration on page 16 and ask the children to circle them with their fingers.

Processing Information

- Children could draw a picture of an animal that lives underground.
- Write captions for the children's drawings, e.g., *This is the* ____.
- Collate the drawings into a book for sharing.

The Monster Town

Setting The Scene

Focus the children's attention on the front cover. Talk about what they can see. Look at the title page. Talk about this.

Reading The Text

Work spread-by-spread through the text up to pages 12-13. Talk about the pictures and what is happening. Read the text to the children. Return to pages 2-3. Focus the children's attention on the text, talking about the starting point. Ask the children to read the text, pointing to the words. Work with one spread at a time. **Make sure that the children match one spoken word to one written word.**

Thinking Critically

- Look at pages 14-15. Ask the children to retell orally what is happening in the picture.
- Ask the children, "Which part of the town would you like to visit and why?" "Why do you think the animals are in the zoo?"

Exploring Language

Terminology: Front, back, cover, title

High-Frequency Words: this, is, the

Phonological Patterns

Focus on initial consonant **p** (**p**ool, **p**ark)

Visual Information

- Focus the children's attention on the caption and labels on pages 14-15. Talk about these.

Word Differentiation

- Focus the children's attention on page 16. Ask the children, "Which monsters want food if the monsters with the words *this, is*, or *the* on them are the hungry ones?"
- Locate the focus words in the illustration on page 16 and ask the children to circle them with their fingers.

Processing Information

- Children could draw a picture of an area in their town.
- Write captions for the children's drawings, e.g., *This is the zoo.*
- Collate the drawings into a book for sharing.

The Pets

Setting The Scene

Focus the children's attention on the front cover. Talk about what they can see. Look at the title page. Talk about this.

Reading The Text

Work spread-by-spread through the text up to pages 12-13. Talk about the pictures and what is happening. Read the text to the children. Return to pages 2-3. Focus the children's attention on the text, talking about the starting point. Ask the children to read the text, pointing to the words. Work with one spread at a time. **Make sure that the children match one spoken word to one written word.**

Thinking Critically

- Look at pages 14-15. Ask the children to retell orally what is happening in the picture.
- Ask the children, "Why do you think the children have numbers on their shirts?" "Why do you think the judge is running away?"

Exploring Language

Terminology: Front, back, cover, title

High-Frequency Words: look, at, the

Phonological Patterns

Focus on initial consonant **d** (**d**uck, **d**og)

Visual Information

- Focus the children's attention on the speech bubble on page 15. Talk about this.

Word Differentiation

- Focus the children's attention on page 16. Ask the children, "Which jars will the children use if they can only use ones with the words *look, at,* or *the* on them?"
- Locate the focus words in the illustration on page 16 and ask the children to circle them with their fingers.

Processing Information

- Children could draw a picture of themselves with a pet that they might like to take to school.
- Write speech bubbles to add to the children's drawings, e.g., *Look at the ____.*
- Collate the drawings into a book for sharing.

Look at the Robot

Setting The Scene

Focus the children's attention on the front cover. Talk about what they can see. Look at the title page. Talk about this.

Reading The Text

Work spread-by-spread through the text up to pages 12-13. Talk about the pictures and what is happening. Read the text to the children. Return to pages 2-3. Focus the children's attention on the text, talking about the starting point. Ask the children to read the text, pointing to the words. Work with one spread at a time. **Make sure that the children match one spoken word to one written word.**

Thinking Critically

- Look at pages 14-15. Ask the children to retell orally what is happening in the picture.
- Ask the children, "Why do you think the big robot is running away?" "Why do you think the little robot is chasing the big robot?"

Exploring Language

Terminology: Front, back, cover, title

High-Frequency Words: look, at, the

Phonological Patterns

Focus on initial consonant **r** (**r**obot)

Visual Information

- Focus the children's attention on the speech bubble on page 14. Talk about this.

Word Differentiation

- Focus the children's attention on page 16. Ask the children, "Which screens will the robot use if it can only use ones with the words *look, at,* or *the* on them?"
- Locate the focus words in the illustration on page 16 and ask the children to circle them with their fingers.

Processing Information

- Children could draw a picture of a robot.
- Write captions for the children's drawings, e.g., *Look at the nose.*
- Collate the drawings into a book for sharing.

Shopping

Setting The Scene

Focus the children's attention on the front cover. Talk about what they can see. Look at the title page. Talk about this.

Reading The Text

Work spread-by-spread through the text up to pages 12-13. Talk about the pictures and what is happening. Read the text to the children. Return to pages 2-3. Focus the children's attention on the text, talking about the starting point. Ask the children to read the text, pointing to the words. Work with one spread at a time. **Make sure that the children match one spoken word to one written word.**

Thinking Critically

- Look at pages 14-15. Ask the children to retell orally what is happening in the pictures.
- Ask the children, "Why do you think the monster's shopping cart tipped over?" "Why do you think all the other monsters are happy?"

Exploring Language

Terminology: Front, back, cover, title

High-Frequency Words: look, at, the

Phonological Patterns
Focus on initial consonant **c** (**c**arrots)

Visual Information
- Focus the children's attention on the storyboard on pages 14-15. Talk about the sequence of the pictures and the speech bubble on page 15.

Word Differentiation
- Focus the children's attention on page 16. Ask the children, "Which apples can the monsters eat if they can only eat ones with the words *look, at,* or *the* on them?"
- Locate the focus words in the illustration on page 16 and ask the children to circle them with their fingers.

Processing Information

- Children could draw a picture of a monster and color it in.
- Write captions for the children's drawings, e.g., *Look at the* green (in green writing) *monster.*
- Collate the drawings into a book for sharing.

Look at the Animals

Setting The Scene

Focus the children's attention on the front cover. Talk about what they can see. Look at the title page. Talk about this.

Reading The Text

Work spread-by-spread through the text up to pages 12-13. Talk about the pictures and what is happening. Read the text to the children. Return to pages 2-3. Focus the children's attention on the text, talking about the starting point. Ask the children to read the text, pointing to the words. Work with one spread at a time. **Make sure that the children match one spoken word to one written word.**

Thinking Critically

- Look at pages 14-15. Ask the children to retell orally what is happening in the picture.
- Ask the children, "Why do you think the animals are in the house?" "Why do you think the rabbit is hiding its eyes?"

Exploring Language

Terminology: Front, back, cover, title

High-Frequency Words: look, at, the

Phonological Patterns

Focus on initial consonant **g** (**g**oat)

Visual Information

- Focus the children's attention on the speech bubble on page 15. Talk about this.

Word Differentiation

- Focus the children's attention on page 16. Ask the children, "Which cans of food will the animals eat if they can only eat ones with the words *look, at,* or *the* on them?"
- Locate the focus words in the illustration on page 16 and ask the children to circle them with their fingers.

Processing Information

- Children could draw a picture of an animal, or cut pictures of animals out of magazines and paste them onto a sheet of paper.
- Write captions for the children's pictures, e.g., *Look at the dog.*
- Collate the pictures into a book for sharing.

The Boat

Setting The Scene

Focus the children's attention on the front cover. Talk about what they can see. Look at the title page. Talk about this.

Reading The Text

Work spread-by-spread through the text up to pages 12-13. Talk about the pictures and what is happening. Read the text to the children. Return to pages 2-3. Focus the children's attention on the text, talking about the starting point. Ask the children to read the text, pointing to the words. Work with one spread at a time. **Make sure that the children match one spoken word to one written word.**

Thinking Critically

- Look at pages 14-15. Ask the children to retell orally what is happening in the pictures.
- Ask the children, "Why do you think the sailor is in the water?" "Where do you think the dolphin will take him?"

Exploring Language

Terminology: Front, back, cover, title

High-Frequency Words: I, can, see, a

Phonological Patterns

Focus on initial consonant **b** (**b**ird, **b**oat)

Visual Information

- Focus the children's attention on the storyboard on pages 14-15. Talk about the sequence of the pictures and the speech bubble on page 15.

Word Differentiation

- Focus the children's attention on page 16. Ask the children, "Which boats will the sailor sail in if he only likes ones with the words *I, can, see,* or *a* on them?"
- Locate the focus words in the illustration on page 16 and ask the children to circle them with their fingers.

Processing Information

- Children could draw a picture of themselves in a boat. They could add one thing to their picture that they might see if they were in a boat.
- Write speech bubbles for the children's drawings, e.g., *I can see a* ____.
- Collate the drawings into a book for sharing.

A House

Setting The Scene

Focus the children's attention on the front cover. Talk about what they can see. Look at the title page. Talk about this.

Reading The Text

Work spread-by-spread through the text up to pages 12-13. Talk about the pictures and what is happening. Read the text to the children. Return to pages 2-3. Focus the children's attention on the text, talking about the starting point. Ask the children to read the text, pointing to the words. Work with one spread at a time. **Make sure that the children match one spoken word to one written word.**

Thinking Critically

- Look at pages 14-15. Ask the children to retell orally what is happening in the picture.
- Ask the children, "What do you think the little monster might be saying to the big monster?" "What do you think will happen next?"

Exploring Language

Terminology: Front, back, cover, title

High-Frequency Words: I, can, see, a

Phonological Patterns
Focus on initial consonant **m** (**m**onster)

Visual Information
- Focus the children's attention on the speech bubble on page 14. Talk about this.

Word Differentiation
- Focus the children's attention on page 16. Ask the children, "Which cakes will the monster eat if it only likes ones with the words *I, can, see,* or *a* on them?"
- Locate the focus words in the illustration on page 16 and ask the children to circle them with their fingers.

Processing Information

- Children could draw a picture of a monster and themselves.
- Write captions for the children's drawings, e.g., *I can see a monster.*
- Collate the drawings into a book for sharing.

The Moon

Setting The Scene

Focus the children's attention on the front cover. Talk about what they can see. Look at the title page. Talk about this.

Reading The Text

Work spread-by-spread through the text up to pages 12-13. Talk about the pictures and what is happening. Read the text to the children. Return to pages 2-3. Focus the children's attention on the text, talking about the starting point. Ask the children to read the text, pointing to the words. Work with one spread at a time. **Make sure that the children match one spoken word to one written word.**

Thinking Critically

- Look at pages 14-15. Ask the children to retell orally what is happening in the pictures.
- Ask the children, "Why do you think the spaceships are racing through space?" "Why do you think the little alien is hiding?"

Exploring Language

Terminology: Front, back, cover, title

High-Frequency Words: I, can, see, the

Phonological Patterns

Focus on initial consonant **m** (**m**oon)

Visual Information

- Focus the children's attention on the storyboard on pages 14-15. Talk about the sequence of the pictures and the speech bubble on page 15.

Word Differentiation

- Focus the children's attention on page 16. Ask the children, "Which spaceships will the alien fly in if it only likes ones with the words *I, can, see,* or *the* on them?"
- Locate the focus words in the illustration on page 16 and ask the children to circle them with their fingers.

Processing Information

- Children could draw a picture of themselves in a spaceship. They can add one thing that they might see from their spaceship.
- Write captions for the children's drawings, e.g., *I can see the stars.*
- Collate the drawings into a book for sharing.

The Balloon Ride

Setting The Scene

Focus the children's attention on the front cover. Talk about what they can see. Look at the title page. Talk about this.

Reading The Text

Work spread-by-spread through the text up to pages 12-13. Talk about the pictures and what is happening. Read the text to the children. Return to pages 2-3. Focus the children's attention on the text, talking about the starting point. Ask the children to read the text, pointing to the words. Work with one spread at a time. **Make sure that the children match one spoken word to one written word.**

Thinking Critically

- Look at pages 14-15. Ask the children to retell orally what is happening in the picture.
- Ask the children, "Why do you think the woman has a telescope?" "Why do you think the woman went to the picnic?"

Exploring Language

Terminology: Front, back, cover, title

High-Frequency Words: I, can, see, the

Phonological Patterns

Focus on initial consonant **p** (**p**eople, **p**icnic)

Visual Information

- Focus the children's attention on the speech bubble on page 14. Talk about this.

Word Differentiation

- Focus the children's attention on page 16. Ask the children, "Which balloons will the spy ride in if she only likes ones with the words *I, can, see,* or *the* on them?"
- Locate the focus words in the illustration on page 16 and ask the children to circle them with their fingers.

Processing Information

- Children could draw a picture of themselves as a spy. They could use magazines to find a picture of something that a spy might see, and cut it out to paste onto their drawing.
- Write speech bubbles for the children's pictures, e.g., *I can see the ____.*
- Collate the pictures into a book for sharing.

In the Mud

Setting The Scene

Focus the children's attention on the front cover. Talk about what they can see. Look at the title page. Talk about this.

Reading The Text

Work spread-by-spread through the text up to pages 12-13. Talk about the pictures and what is happening. Read the text to the children. Return to pages 2-3. Focus the children's attention on the text, talking about the starting point. Ask the children to read the text, pointing to the words. Work with one spread at a time. **Make sure that the children match one spoken word to one written word.**

Thinking Critically

- Look at pages 14-15. Ask the children to retell orally what is happening in the pictures.
- Ask the children, "Where do you think the monster will go next?" "If the monster didn't have a bath, what do you think might happen?"

Exploring Language

Terminology: Front, back, cover, title

High-Frequency Words: I, went, in, the

Phonological Patterns

Focus on initial consonant **m** (**m**ud)

Visual Information

- Focus the children's attention on the flow chart on pages 14-15. Talk about the sequence of the pictures and the speech bubble on page 14.

Word Differentiation

- Focus the children's attention on page 16. Ask the children, "Which toys will the monster play with if it only likes the ones with the words *I, went, in,* or *the* on them?"
- Locate the focus words in the illustration on page 16 and ask the children to circle them with their fingers.

Processing Information

- Children could draw a picture of themselves going into something.
- Write captions for the children's drawings, e.g., *I went in the ____.*
- Collate the drawings into a book for sharing.

The Snake

Setting The Scene

Focus the children's attention on the front cover. Talk about what they can see. Look at the title page. Talk about this.

Reading The Text

Work spread-by-spread through the text up to pages 12-13. Talk about the pictures and what is happening. Read the text to the children. Return to pages 2-3. Focus the children's attention on the text, talking about the starting point. Ask the children to read the text, pointing to the words. Work with one spread at a time. **Make sure that the children match one spoken word to one written word.**

Thinking Critically

- Look at pages 14-15. Ask the children to retell orally what is happening in the pictures.
- Ask the children, "Why do you think the man put the snake in the box?" "Why do you think the snake is in the tree?"

Exploring Language

Terminology: Front, back, cover, title

High-Frequency Words: I, went, in, the

Phonological Patterns
Focus on initial consonant **s** (**s**ock)

Visual Information
- Focus the children's attention on the storyboard on pages 14-15. Talk about the sequence of the pictures and the speech bubble on page 14.

Word Differentiation
- Focus the children's attention on page 16. Ask the children, "Which things will the snake choose to sleep in if it only likes the ones with the words *I, went, in,* or *the* on them?"
- Locate the focus words in the illustration on page 16 and ask the children to circle them with their fingers.

Processing Information

- Children could draw a picture of a snake sliding into something.
- Write speech bubbles for the children's drawings, e.g., *I went in the* ____.
- Collate the drawings into a book for sharing.

My Trip

Setting The Scene

Focus the children's attention on the front cover. Talk about what they can see. Look at the title page. Talk about this.

Reading The Text

Work spread-by-spread through the text up to pages 12-13. Talk about the pictures and what is happening. Read the text to the children. Return to pages 2-3. Focus the children's attention on the text, talking about the starting point. Ask the children to read the text, pointing to the words. Work with one spread at a time. **Make sure that the children match one spoken word to one written word.**

Thinking Critically

- Look at pages 14-15. Ask the children to retell orally what is happening in the pictures.
- Ask the children, "Which place do you think is the best place for the alien to go?" "Where do you think the alien might go now?"

Exploring Language

Terminology: Front, back, cover, title

High-Frequency Words: I, went, to, the

Phonological Patterns
Focus on initial consonant **j** (**j**ungle)

Visual Information
- Focus the children's attention on the flow chart on pages 14-15. Talk about the sequence of the pictures and the speech bubble on page 14.

Word Differentiation
- Focus the children's attention on page 16. Ask the children, "Which places will the alien revisit if it only liked ones with the words *I, went, to,* or *the* on them?"
- Locate the focus words in the illustration on page 16 and ask the children to circle them with their fingers.

Processing Information

- Children could draw a picture of an alien showing a place it visited.
- Put the pictures together in a flow chart. Add captions or speech bubbles, e.g., *I went to the ____.*
- Make a cover for the flow chart with the title: "Come and Read Our Flow Chart."

The Bird

Setting The Scene

Focus the children's attention on the front cover. Talk about what they can see. Look at the title page. Talk about this.

Reading The Text

Work spread-by-spread through the text up to pages 12-13. Talk about the pictures and what is happening. Read the text to the children. Return to pages 2-3. Focus the children's attention on the text, talking about the starting point. Ask the children to read the text, pointing to the words. Work with one spread at a time. **Make sure that the children match one spoken word to one written word.**

Thinking Critically

- Look at pages 14-15. Ask the children to retell orally what is happening in the pictures.
- Ask the children, "Why do you think the bird doesn't look happy in the bird bath?" "What do you think might happen to the bird in the swimming pool?"

Exploring Language

Terminology: Front, back, cover, title

High-Frequency Words: I, went, to, the

Phonological Patterns

Focus on initial consonant **p** (**p**ool)

Visual Information

- Focus the children's attention on the storyboard on pages 14-15. Talk about the sequence of the pictures and the speech bubble on page 15.

Word Differentiation

- Focus the children's attention on page 16. Ask the children, "Which bowls of birdseed will the bird eat if it can only eat ones with the words *I, went, to,* or *the* on them?"
- Locate the focus words in the illustration on page 16 and ask the children to circle them with their fingers.

Processing Information

- Children could draw a picture of a place they have visited.
- Write captions for the children's drawings, e.g., *I went to the ____.*
- Collate the drawings into a book for sharing.

The Mice

Setting the Scene

Focus the children's attention on the front cover. Talk about what they can see. Look at the title page. Talk about this.

Reading the Text

Work spread-by-spread through the text up to pages 12-13. Talk about the pictures and what is happening. Read the text to the children. Return to pages 2-3. Focus the children's attention on the text, talking about the starting point. Ask the children to read the text, pointing to the words. Work with one spread at a time. **Make sure that the children match one spoken word to one written word.**

Thinking Critically

- Look at pages 14-15. Ask the children to retell orally what is happening in the pictures.
- Ask the children, "Why do you think the mice are in the girl's hood?" "What do you think might happen if the girl sees the mice?"

Exploring Language

Terminology: Front, back, cover, title

High-Frequency Words: we, went, in, the

Phonological Patterns

Focus on initial consonant **b** (**b**ox, **b**ucket)

Visual Information

- Focus the children's attention on the storyboard on pages 14-15. Talk about the sequence of the pictures and the speech bubble on page 15.

Word Differentiation

- Focus the children's attention on page 16. Ask the children, "Which cheese will the mice choose if they can only choose ones with the words *we, went, in,* or *the* on them?"
- Locate the focus words in the illustration on page 16 and ask the children to circle them with their fingers.

Processing Information

- Children could draw a picture of themselves and a friend hiding somewhere.
- Write captions for the children's drawings, e.g., *We went in the ____.*
- Collate the drawings into a book for sharing.

The Bears

Setting The Scene

Focus the children's attention on the front cover. Talk about what they can see. Look at the title page. Talk about this.

Reading The Text

Work spread-by-spread through the text up to pages 12-13. Talk about the pictures and what is happening. Read the text to the children. Return to pages 2-3. Focus the children's attention on the text, talking about the starting point. Ask the children to read the text, pointing to the words. Work with one spread at a time. **Make sure that the children match one spoken word to one written word.**

Thinking Critically

- Look at pages 14-15. Ask the children to retell orally what is happening in the picture.
- Ask the children, "Where do you think the bears might be going?" "Why do you think the car is there?"

Exploring Language

Terminology: Front, back, cover, title

High-Frequency Words: we, went, in, the

Phonological Patterns
Focus on initial consonant **c** (**c**ar, **c**ave)

Visual Information
- Focus the children's attention on the trail on pages 14-15 and track the bears' path. Talk about the speech bubble on page 15.

Word Differentiation
- Focus the children's attention on page 16. Ask the children, "Which dishes will the bears choose if they can only choose ones with the words *we, went, in,* or *the* on them?"
- Locate the focus words in the illustration on page 16 and ask the children to circle them with their fingers.

Processing Information

- Children could draw a picture of themselves and a friend going away in something.
- Write captions for the children's drawings, e.g., *We went in the ____.*
- Collate the drawings into a book for sharing.

The Vacation

Setting The Scene

Focus the children's attention on the front cover. Talk about what they can see. Look at the title page. Talk about this.

Reading The Text

Work spread-by-spread through the text up to pages 12-13. Talk about the pictures and what is happening. Read the text to the children. Return to pages 2-3. Focus the children's attention on the text, talking about the starting point. Ask the children to read the text, pointing to the words. Work with one spread at a time. **Make sure that the children match one spoken word to one written word.**

Thinking Critically

- Look at pages 14-15. Ask the children to retell orally what is happening in the pictures.
- Ask the children, "Why do you think the dragons are going to the mountains?" "Why do you think the dragons have suitcases?"

Exploring Language

Terminology: Front, back, cover, title

High-Frequency Words: we, went, to, the

Phonological Patterns

Focus on initial consonant **p** (**p**ark)

Visual Information

- Focus the children's attention on the two-frame storyboard on pages 14-15. Talk about the sequence of the pictures and the speech bubble on page 14.

Word Differentiation

- Focus the children's attention on page 16. Ask the children, "Which bags belong to the dragons if theirs are the ones with the words *we, went, to,* or *the* on them?"
- Locate the focus words in the illustration on page 16 and ask the children to circle them with their fingers.

Processing Information

- Children could draw a picture of themselves and their family going somewhere.
- Write captions for the children's drawings, e.g., *We went to the ____.*
- Collate the drawings into a book for sharing.

Our Day

Setting The Scene

Focus the children's attention on the front cover. Talk about what they can see. Look at the title page. Talk about this.

Reading The Text

Work spread-by-spread through the text up to pages 12-13. Talk about the pictures and what is happening. Read the text to the children. Return to pages 2-3. Focus the children's attention on the text, talking about the starting point. Ask the children to read the text, pointing to the words. Work with one spread at a time. **Make sure that the children match one spoken word to one written word.**

Thinking Critically

- Look at pages 14-15. Ask the children to retell orally what is happening in the picture.
- Ask the children, "Why do you think the animals are peeping through the window?" "Why do you think the bears are in the hospital?"

Exploring Language

Terminology: Front, back, cover, title

High-Frequency Words: we, went, to, the

Phonological Patterns
Focus on initial consonant **p** (**p**arty, **p**icnic)

Visual Information
- Focus the children's attention on the speech bubble and signs on pages 14-15. Talk about their information.

Word Differentiation
- Focus the children's attention on page 16. Ask the children, "Which party things will the bears choose if they can only choose ones with the words *we, went, to,* or *the* on them?"
- Locate the focus words in the illustration on page 16 and ask the children to circle them with their fingers.

Processing Information

- Children could draw a picture of themselves going somewhere with a friend.
- Write captions for the children's drawings, e.g., *We went to the ____.* (Add a picture clue to the caption if necessary.)
- Collate the drawings into a book for sharing.

My Hat

Setting The Scene

Focus the children's attention on the front cover. Talk about what they can see. Look at the title page. Talk about this.

Reading The Text

Work spread-by-spread through the text up to pages 12-13. Talk about the pictures and what is happening. Read the text to the children. Return to pages 2-3. Focus the children's attention on the text, talking about the starting point. Ask the children to read the text, pointing to the words. Work with one spread at a time. **Make sure that the children match one spoken word to one written word.**

Thinking Critically

- Look at pages 14-15. Ask the children to retell orally what is happening in the pictures.
- Ask the children, "Why do you think the little sailor is pointing to the big sailor?" "What do you think the sailors will do with their clothes?"

Exploring Language

Terminology: Front, back, cover, title

High-Frequency Words: I, put, on, my

Phonological Patterns
Focus on initial consonant **h** (**h**at)

Visual Information
- Focus the children's attention on the storyboard on pages 14-15. Talk about the sequence of the pictures and the speech bubble on page 15.

Word Differentiation
- Focus the children's attention on page 16. Ask the children, "Which boats will the sailors sail in if they can only sail ones with the words *I, put, on,* or *my* on them?"
- Locate the focus words in the illustration on page 16 and ask the children to circle them with their fingers.

Processing Information

- Children could draw a picture of themselves getting dressed.
- Write speech bubbles for the children's drawings, e.g., *I put on my____.*
- Collate the drawings into a book for sharing.

The Spy

Setting The Scene

Focus the children's attention on the front cover. Talk about what they can see. Look at the title page. Talk about this.

Reading The Text

Work spread-by-spread through the text up to pages 12-13. Talk about the pictures and what is happening. Read the text to the children. Return to pages 2-3. Focus the children's attention on the text, talking about the starting point. Ask the children to read the text, pointing to the words. Work with one spread at a time. **Make sure that the children match one spoken word to one written word.**

Thinking Critically

- Look at pages 14-15. Ask the children to retell orally what is happening in the pictures.
- Ask the children, "Why do you think the spy is spying on the bird?" "What do you think the spy is thinking when the bird takes his hair?"

Exploring Language

Terminology: Front, back, cover, title

High-Frequency Words: I, put, on, my

Phonological Patterns

Focus on initial consonant **h** (**h**at, **h**air)

Visual Information

- Focus the children's attention on the storyboard on pages 14-15. Talk about the sequence of the pictures and the speech bubble on page 15.

Word Differentiation

- Focus the children's attention on page 16. Ask the children, "Which wigs will the spy wear if he can only wear ones with the words *I, put, on,* or *my* on them?"
- Locate the focus words in the illustration on page 16 and ask the children to circle them with their fingers.

Processing Information

- Children could draw a picture of themselves as a spy, choosing the "spy gear" they would like to wear.
- Write captions for the children's drawings, e.g., *I put on my hat.*
- Collate the drawings into a book for sharing.

The Race Car

Setting the Scene

Focus the children's attention on the front cover. Talk about what they can see. Look at the title page. Talk about this.

Reading the Text

Work spread-by-spread through the text up to pages 12-13. Talk about the pictures and what is happening. Read the text to the children. Return to pages 2-3. Focus the children's attention on the text, talking about the starting point. Ask the children to read the text, pointing to the words. Work with one spread at a time. **Make sure that the children match one spoken word to one written word.**

Thinking Critically

- Look at pages 14-15. Ask the children to retell orally what is happening in the picture.
- Ask the children, "What do you think might happen if the monsters go over the bridge?" "What do you think the monsters will do now?"

Exploring Language

Terminology: Front, back, cover, title

High-Frequency Words: we, put, on, the

Phonological Patterns
Focus on initial consonant **r** (**r**oof)

Visual Information
- Focus the children's attention on the trail on pages 14-15. Talk about the trail's information and the speech bubble on page 15.

Word Differentiation
- Focus the children's attention on page 16. Ask the children, "Which tires would the monsters choose if they only wanted ones with the words *we, put, on,* or *the* on them?"
- Locate the focus words in the illustration on page 16 and ask the children to circle them with their fingers.

Processing Information

- Children could draw a picture of themselves and a friend making a race car.
- Write captions for the children's drawings, e.g., *We put on the ____.*
- Collate the drawings into a book for sharing.

The Snowman

Setting The Scene

Focus the children's attention on the front cover. Talk about what they can see. Look at the title page. Talk about this.

Reading The Text

Work spread-by-spread through the text up to pages 12-13. Talk about the pictures and what is happening. Read the text to the children. Return to pages 2-3. Focus the children's attention on the text, talking about the starting point. Ask the children to read the text, pointing to the words. Work with one spread at a time. **Make sure that the children match one spoken word to one written word.**

Thinking Critically

- Look at pages 14-15. Ask the children to retell orally what is happening in the picture on page 15.
- Ask the children, "Where do you think the snowman might go?" "What might the squirrels be thinking?"

Exploring Language

Terminology: Front, back, cover, title

High-Frequency Words: we, put, on, the

Phonological Patterns

Focus on initial consonant **h** (**h**ead, **h**at)

Visual Information

- Focus the children's attention on the storyboard on pages 14-15. Talk about the sequence of the pictures.

Word Differentiation

- Focus the children's attention on page 16. Ask the children, "Which snowballs will the squirrels use for a snowman if they can only use ones with the words *we, put, on,* or *the* on them?"
- Locate the focus words in the illustration on page 16 and ask the children to circle them with their fingers.

Processing Information

- Children could draw a picture of themselves and a friend putting something on a snowman.
- Write captions for the children's drawings, e.g., *We put on the ____.*
- Collate the drawings into a book for sharing.

I Like Jam

Setting The Scene

Focus the children's attention on the front cover. Talk about what they can see. Look at the title page. Talk about this.

Reading The Text

Work spread-by-spread through the text up to pages 12-13. Talk about the pictures and what is happening. Read the text to the children. Return to pages 2-3. Focus the children's attention on the text, talking about the starting point. Ask the children to read the text, pointing to the words. Work with one spread at a time. **Make sure that the children match one spoken word to one written word.**

Thinking Critically

- Look at pages 14-15. Ask the children to retell orally what is happening in the pictures.
- Ask the children, "How do you think the monster will feel if he can only have ice cream?" "What do you think the monster will do with the jam and bugs?"

Exploring Language

Terminology: Front, back, cover, title

High-Frequency Words: I, like, and

Phonological Patterns

Focus on initial consonant **b** (**b**ones)

Visual Information

- Focus the children's attention on the illustrative text and speech bubble on pages 14-15. Talk about these.

Word Differentiation

- Focus the children's attention on page 16. Ask the children, "Which jars of jam will the monster choose if it can only choose ones with the words *I, like,* or *and* on them?"
- Locate the focus words in the illustration on page 16 and ask the children to circle them with their fingers.

Processing Information

- Children could draw a picture of themselves putting jam on something they like.
- Write captions for the children's drawings, e.g., *I like jam and ____.*
- Collate the drawings into a book for sharing.

Rainbow Town

SETTING THE SCENE

Focus the children's attention on the front cover. Talk about what they can see. Look at the title page. Talk about this.

READING THE TEXT

Work spread-by-spread through the text up to pages 12-13. Talk about the pictures and what is happening. Read the text to the children. Return to pages 2-3. Focus the children's attention on the text, talking about the starting point. Ask the children to read the text, pointing to the words. Work with one spread at a time. **Make sure that the children match one spoken word to one written word.**

THINKING CRITICALLY

- Look at pages 14-15. Ask the children to retell orally what is happening in the pictures.
- Ask the children, "Why do you think the town is called Rainbow Town?" "What do you think will happen to the houses when the rain stops?"

EXPLORING LANGUAGE

Terminology: Front, back, cover, title

High-Frequency Words: I, like, and

Phonological Patterns

Focus on initial consonant **r** (**r**ed)

Visual Information

- Focus the children's attention on the storyboard on pages 14-15. Talk about the sequence of the pictures and the thought bubble on page 14.

Word Differentiation

- Focus the children's attention on page 16. Ask the children, "Which cans of paint will the people use if they can only buy ones with the words *I, like,* or *and* on them?"
- Locate the focus words in the illustration on page 16 and ask the children to circle them with their fingers.

PROCESSING INFORMATION

- Children could draw a picture of a different house they would like to live in and choose two colors to paint it with.
- Write captions for the children's drawings, e.g., *I like ____ and ____.*
- Collate the drawings into a book for sharing.

I Like Boxes

Setting The Scene

Focus the children's attention on the front cover. Talk about what they can see. Look at the title page. Talk about this.

Reading The Text

Work spread-by-spread through the text up to pages 12-13. Talk about the pictures and what is happening. Read the text to the children. Return to pages 2-3. Focus the children's attention on the text, talking about the starting point. Ask the children to read the text, pointing to the words. Work with one spread at a time. **Make sure that the children match one spoken word to one written word.**

Thinking Critically

- Look at pages 14-15. Ask the children to retell orally what is happening in the picture.
- Ask the children, "Which box do you think would be the best box for a mouse to live in?" "Why do you think boxes might not be good places for mice to live in?"

Exploring Language

Terminology: Front, back, cover, title

High-Frequency Words: I, like, and

Phonological Patterns

Focus on initial consonant **b** (**b**oxes, **b**eans)

Visual Information

- Focus the children's attention on the speech bubble on page 15. Talk about this.

Word Differentiation

- Focus the children's attention on page 16. Ask the children, "Which boxes will the mice use if they can only choose ones with the words *I, like,* or *and* on them?"
- Locate the focus words in the illustration on page 16 and ask the children to circle them with their fingers.

Processing Information

- Children could draw a picture of themselves. They could use magazines to find pictures of two things that they like, and cut them out to paste onto their drawing.
- Write captions for the children's pictures, e.g., *I like ice cream and cake.*
- Collate the pictures into a book for sharing.

Hats

Setting The Scene

Focus the children's attention on the front cover. Talk about what they can see. Look at the title page. Talk about this.

Reading The Text

Work spread-by-spread through the text up to pages 12-13. Talk about the pictures and what is happening. Read the text to the children. Return to pages 2-3. Focus the children's attention on the text, talking about the starting point. Ask the children to read the text, pointing to the words. Work with one spread at a time. **Make sure that the children match one spoken word to one written word.**

Thinking Critically

- Look at pages 14-15. Ask the children to retell orally what is happening in the picture.
- Ask the children, "Why do you think all the bears are wearing hats?" "Which hat do you think will win the prize? Why?"

Exploring Language

Terminology: Front, back, cover, title

High-Frequency Words: I, like, and

Phonological Patterns

Focus on initial consonant **f** (**f**eathers, **f**ish)

Visual Information

- Focus the children's attention on the speech bubble on page 15. Talk about this.

Word Differentiation

- Focus the children's attention on page 16. Ask the children, "If the judge only likes hats with the words *I, like,* or *and* on them, which ones would he vote for?"
- Locate the focus words in the illustration on page 16 and ask the children to circle them with their fingers.

Processing Information

- Children could draw a picture of themselves wearing a hat. They could put something interesting on their hat.
- Write speech bubbles for the children's drawings, e.g., *I like hats and ____.*
- Collate the drawings into a book for sharing.

The Presents

Setting The Scene

Focus the children's attention on the front cover. Talk about what they can see. Look at the title page. Talk about this.

Reading The Text

Work spread-by-spread through the text up to pages 12-13. Talk about the pictures and what is happening. Read the text to the children. Return to pages 2-3. Focus the children's attention on the text, talking about the starting point. Ask the children to read the text, pointing to the words. Work with one spread at a time. **Make sure that the children match one spoken word to one written word.**

Thinking Critically

- Look at pages 14-15. Ask the children to retell orally what is happening in the picture.
- Ask the children, "Why do you think the characters look happy?" "Why do you think the spy is looking at the food with his magnifying glass?"

Exploring Language

Terminology: Front, back, cover, title

High-Frequency Words: this, is, for, a

Phonological Patterns

Focus on initial consonant **r** (**r**obot)

Visual Information

- Focus the children's attention on the label on page 14. Talk about this.

Word Differentiation

- Focus the children's attention on page 16. Ask the children, "Which wrapping paper would the robot choose if it only liked ones with the words *this, is, for,* or *a* on them?"
- Locate the focus words in the illustration on page 16 and ask the children to circle them with their fingers.

Processing Information

- Children could draw a picture of a present.
- Write labels for the children's drawings, e.g., *This is for a ____.*
- Collate the drawings into a book for sharing.

Dinner

Setting The Scene

Focus the children's attention on the front cover. Talk about what they can see. Look at the title page. Talk about this.

Reading The Text

Work spread-by-spread through the text up to pages 12-13. Talk about the pictures and what is happening. Read the text to the children. Return to pages 2-3. Focus the children's attention on the text, talking about the starting point. Ask the children to read the text, pointing to the words. Work with one spread at a time. **Make sure that the children match one spoken word to one written word.**

Thinking Critically

- Look at pages 14-15. Ask the children to retell orally what is happening in the pictures.
- Ask the children, "Why do you think the farmer is using the wheelbarrow?" "Why do you think the monster looks happy?"

Exploring Language

Terminology: Front, back, cover, title

High-Frequency Words: this, is, for, a

Phonological Patterns

Focus on initial consonant **d** (**d**og, **d**uck)

Visual Information

- Focus the children's attention on the storyboard on pages 14-15. Talk about the sequence of the pictures and the speech bubble on page 15.

Word Differentiation

- Focus the children's attention on page 16. Ask the children, "Which buckets of food will the monster choose if it can only choose ones with the words *this, is, for,* or *a* on them?"
- Locate the focus words in the illustration on page 16 and ask the children to circle them with their fingers.

Processing Information

- Children could draw a picture of something a monster would like to eat.
- Write captions for the children's drawings, e.g., *This is for a monster.* Add labels to the pictures, e.g., *a banana, a cookie.*
- Collate the drawings into a book for sharing.

Wheels

Setting The Scene

Focus the children's attention on the front cover. Talk about what they can see. Look at the title page. Talk about this.

Reading The Text

Work spread-by-spread through the text up to pages 12-13. Talk about the pictures and what is happening. Read the text to the children. Return to pages 2-3. Focus the children's attention on the text, talking about the starting point. Ask the children to read the text, pointing to the words. Work with one spread at a time. **Make sure that the children match one spoken word to one written word.**

Thinking Critically

- Look at pages 14-15. Ask the children to retell orally what is happening in the pictures.
- Ask the children, "Why do you think the monster was lucky?" "What do you think will happen to the monster's plane?"

Exploring Language

Terminology: Front, back, cover, title

High-Frequency Words: this, is, for, the

Phonological Patterns

Focus on initial consonant **b** (**b**us, **b**ike)

Visual Information

- Focus the children's attention on the storyboard on pages 14-15. Talk about the sequence of the pictures and the label on page 14.

Word Differentiation

- Focus the children's attention on page 16. Ask the children, "Which wheels will the monster choose if it can only choose ones with the words *this, is, for,* or *the* on them?"
- Locate the focus words in the illustration on page 16 and ask the children to circle them with their fingers.

Processing Information

- Fold a piece of paper in half so that the children can draw a wheel on the first half. On the second half, ask the children to draw a picture of something that the wheel could go on.
- Write captions for the children's drawings, e.g., *This is for the ___.*
- Collate the drawings into a book for sharing.

The New House

Setting The Scene

Focus the children's attention on the front cover. Talk about what they can see. Look at the title page. Talk about this.

Reading The Text

Work spread-by-spread through the text up to pages 12-13. Talk about the pictures and what is happening. Read the text to the children. Return to pages 2-3. Focus the children's attention on the text, talking about the starting point. Ask the children to read the text, pointing to the words. Work with one spread at a time. **Make sure that the children match one spoken word to one written word.**

Thinking Critically

- Look at pages 14-15. Ask the children to retell orally what is happening in the picture.
- Ask the children, "Why do you think the kitchen was not a good place to have the bathtub?" "Which room do you think the robot likes best? Why?"

Exploring Language

Terminology: Front, back, cover, title

High-Frequency Words: this, is, for, the

Phonological Patterns

Focus on initial consonant **b** (**b**edroom, **b**athroom)

Visual Information

- Focus the children's attention on the labels on pages 14-15. Talk about these.

Word Differentiation

- Focus the children's attention on page 16. Ask the children, "If the robot only likes lamps with the words *this, is, for,* or *the* on them, which ones will it choose?"
- Locate the focus words in the illustration on page 16 and ask the children to circle them with their fingers.

Processing Information

- Children could draw a picture of a house. They could use magazines to find a picture of something that could be put in their house, and cut it out to paste onto their drawing.
- Write captions for the children's drawings, e.g., *This is for the* ____.
- Collate the pictures into a book for sharing.

Assessment and Evaluation

First Wave: Beginning Level

Oral Language

Check: Beginning *(To be achieved by completion of First Wave: Beginning Level.)*	
Can talk about a story from a storyboard or visual.	
Can talk about responses to a text.	
Can express an opinion.	
Is extending and enriching spoken vocabulary.	

Observations

Date and record any relevant observations:

Note: This is a check only for targets that are introduced and reinforced through the *First Wave: Beginning Level* books.

Written Language: Writing

Check: Beginning *(To be achieved by completion of First Wave: Beginning Level.)*	
Can write some simple high-frequency words.	

Observations

Date and record any relevant observations:

Note: This is a check only for targets that are introduced and reinforced through the *First Wave: Beginning Level* books.

Written Language: Reading

Check: Beginning *(To be achieved by completion of First Wave: Beginning Level.)*	
Can find the cover, back, and spine of book and turn the pages correctly.	
Can identify where to start reading.	
Can demonstrate correct directional movement.	
Can match one spoken word to one written word.	
Can talk about a story using visual information (pictures).	
Can tell something about the characters in the story.	
Can interpret illustrations to predict text.	
Can recognize some high-frequency words.	
Can make inferences from illustrations.	
Can identify some initial consonants.	
Can identify a word and a letter.	
Can match words that are the same: to here is the look here look the is me to me	
Can recognize similarities in words: he saw look went like said me here my	
Can read the sentence under the picture: Here is a house.	

Visual Language

Check: Beginning *(To be achieved by completion of First Wave: Beginning Level.)*

Can look at simple visual information in the text and talk about the meaning.	

Observations

Date and record any relevant observations:

Note: This is a check only for targets that are introduced and reinforced through the *First Wave: Beginning Level* books.

Phonological Patterns

Check: Beginning *(To be achieved by completion of First Wave: Beginning Level.)*	
Can see similarities in some words and can match letters and words.	
Knows the names of some letters.	
Knows the sounds represented by some initial consonants.	
Can recognize the difference between a letter and a word.	

Observations

Date and record any relevant observations:

Note: This is a check only for targets that are introduced and reinforced through the *First Wave: Beginning Level* books.

High-Frequency Words

Check: *Beginning*

a	the	is	my	I
can	like	am	here	this
look	can	see	went	in
to	put	on	and	for
at				

Score:

Word Power

Check: *Beginning*

How many words can you write?

Score:
(5 minutes)

Assessment Task: Phonological Patterns – Initial Consonants

Beginning

Draw a line between the letters that match.

b	m
t	l
l	t
m	b

Evaluation
Goals:

Assessment Task: Phonological Patterns – Initial Consonants

Beginning

Draw a line between the letters that match.	
h	d
p	s
s	p
d	h

Evaluation

Goals:

Assessment Task: Phonological Patterns – Recognizing Similarities in Words

Beginning

Draw a line between the words that match.

a	the
the	am
am	I
I	a

Evaluation
Goals:

Assessment Task: Phonological Patterns – Recognizing Similarities in Words

Beginning

Draw a line between the words that match.

here	look
is	this
this	is
look	here

Evaluation

Goals:

Independent Reinforcement Activities

First Wave: Beginning Level

WRITING
CUTTING and PASTING
Independent Reinforcement
FOCUS WORDS Here is the
Use the focus words to complete the caption.
is the Here
monkey
bear
Here is a
Here
is
dog
Independent Reinforcement Activity
FOCUS WORDS I can
Cut out the focus words and paste them in the correct order on the blank lines.
I can
swim.
fly.
to
A
I
can
can
Independent Reinforcement Activity
FOCUS WORDS I can
Use the focus words to complete the speech bubbles.
I can
meow.
squeak.

Independent Reinforcement Activity

CUTTING and PASTING

FOCUS WORD a

Cut out the words below and paste them into the correct box.

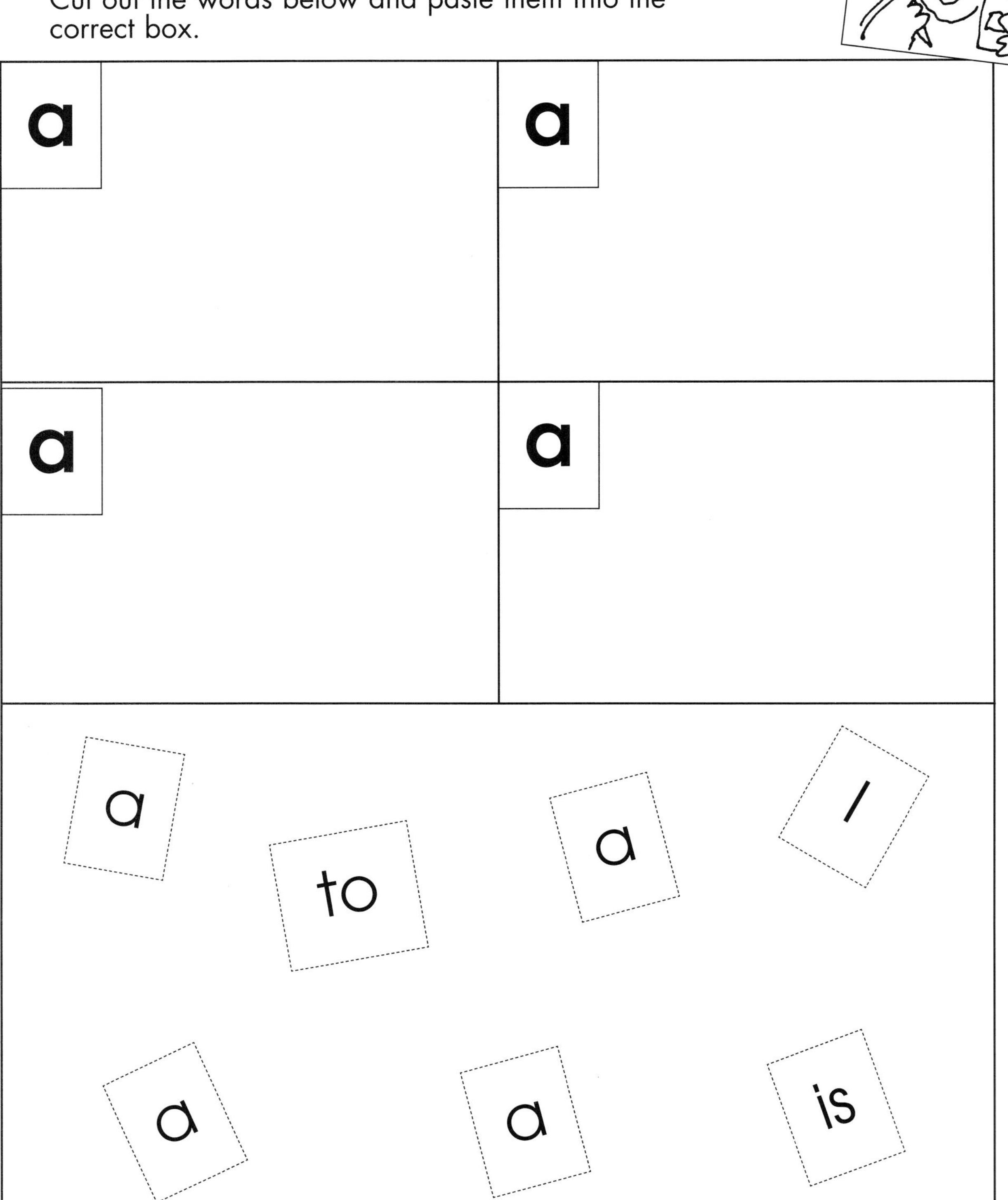

Titles: A Garden • A Monster House • A Ride • A Home

Independent Reinforcement Activity

WRITING

FOCUS WORD **a**

Complete the labels on the picture.

a

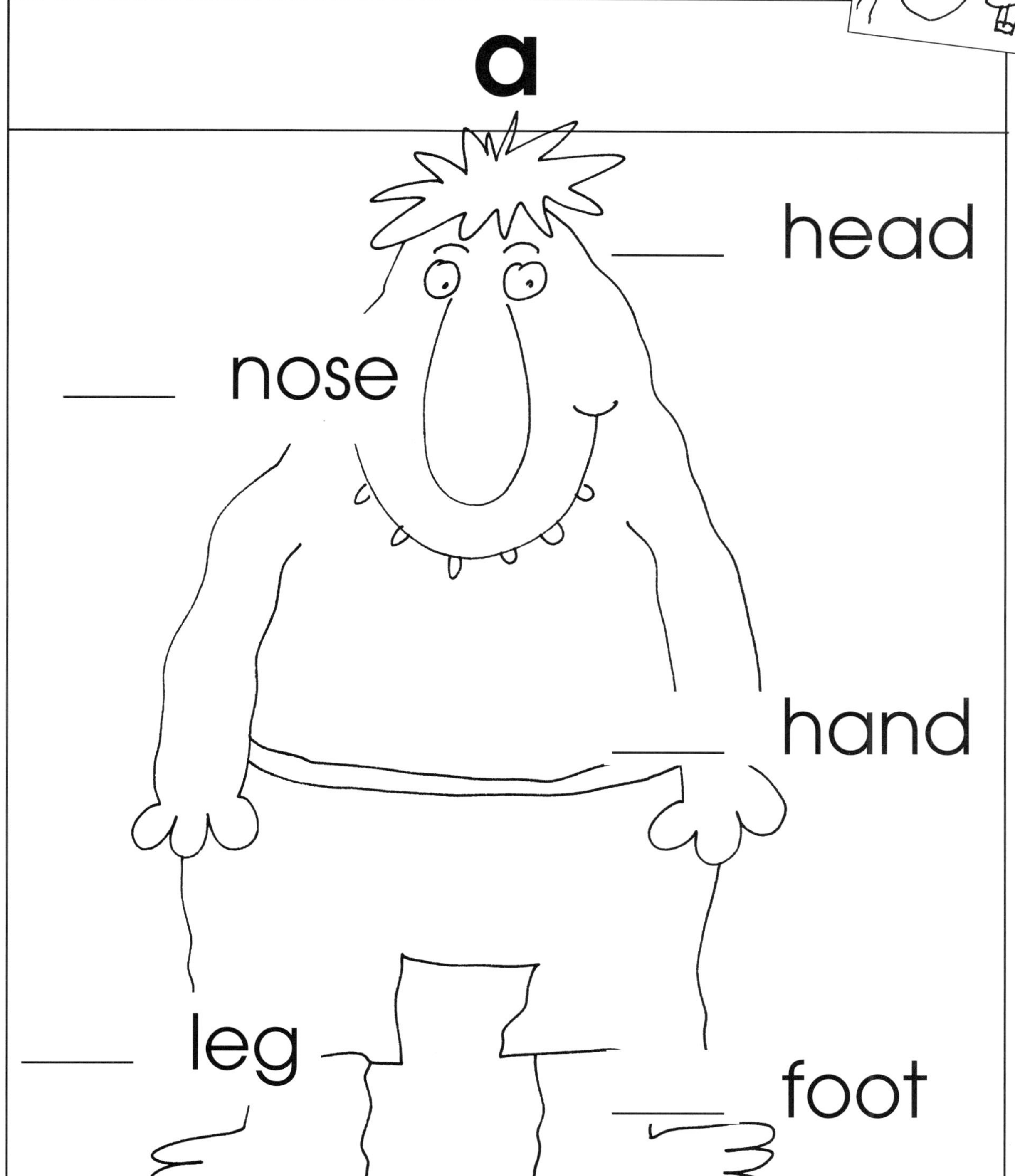

Titles: A Garden • A Monster House • A Ride • A Home

Independent Reinforcement Activity

FOCUS WORD the

Cut out the letters belonging to the focus word and paste them in the correct order in the empty boxes.

the	
the	

t e h r s i h t a e

Titles: The Jungle • The Farm • The Day • The Monster's Clothes

Independent Reinforcement Activity

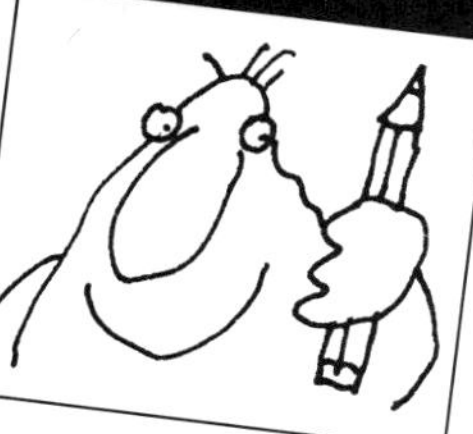

FOCUS WORD the

Complete the labels on the picture.

the

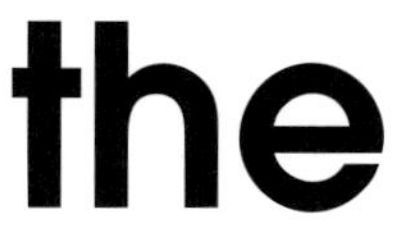

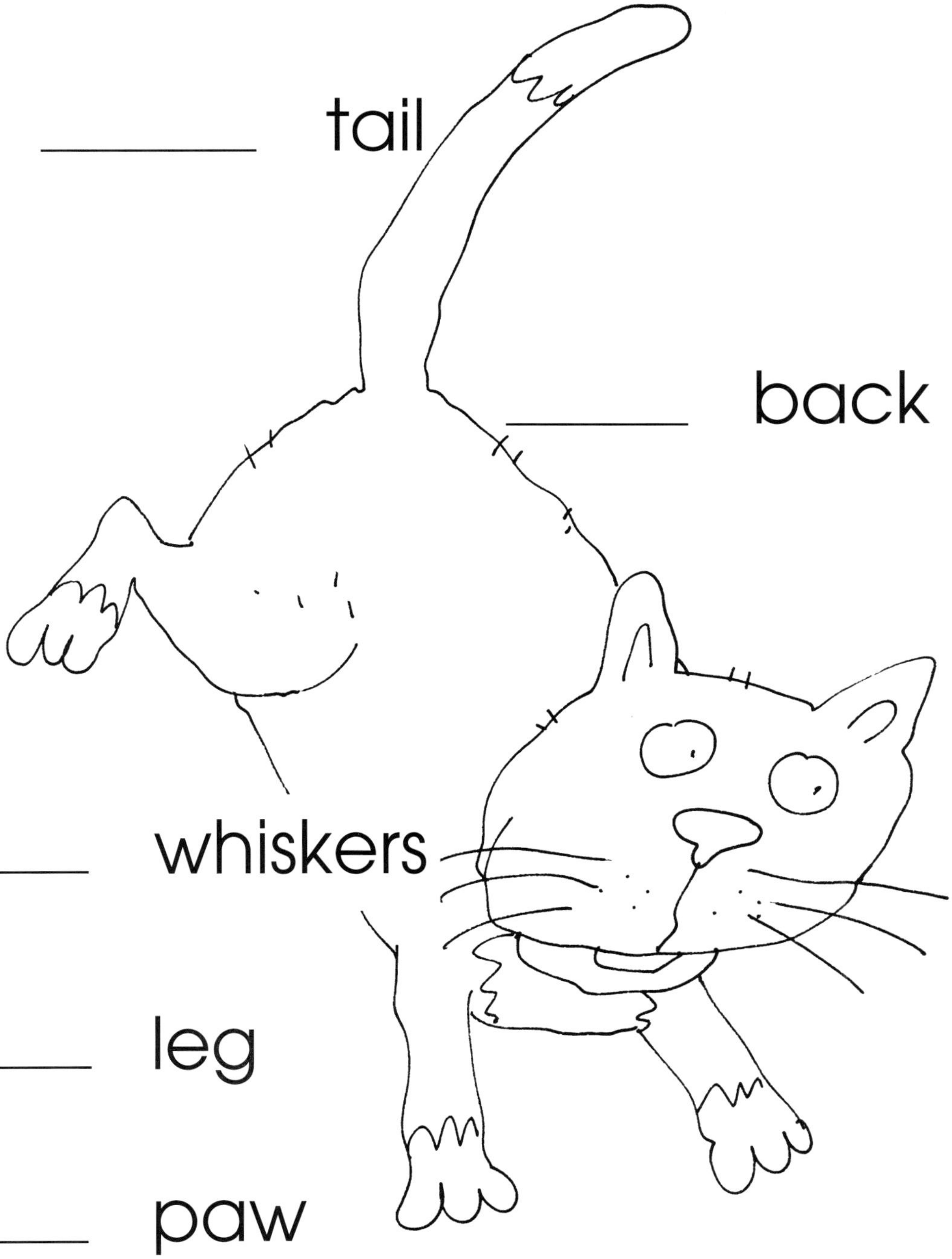

______ tail

______ back

______ whiskers

______ leg

______ paw

Titles: The Jungle • The Farm • The Day • The Monster's Clothes

Independent Reinforcement Activity

FOCUS WORD my

Cut out the letters belonging to the focus word and paste them in the correct order in the boxes.

my	my

m y A r y h m t

Titles: My Clothes • My Family • My Alien • My Things

Independent Reinforcement Activity

FOCUS WORD **my**

Complete the labels on the picture.

my

________ hat

________ hair

________ nose

________ pants

________ shoe

________ sock

Titles: My Clothes • My Family • My Alien • My Things

Independent Reinforcement Activity

FOCUS WORDS I can

Cut out the focus words and paste them in the correct order on the blank lines.

I can

_____ __________ swim.

_____ __________ fly.

to A I / can can

Titles: I Can • I Can Laugh • The Animals • I Can Swim

Independent Reinforcement Activity

FOCUS WORDS **I can**

Use the focus words to complete the speech bubbles.

I can

___ _______ meow.

___ _______ squeak.

Titles: I Can • I Can Laugh • The Animals • I Can Swim

Independent Reinforcement Activity

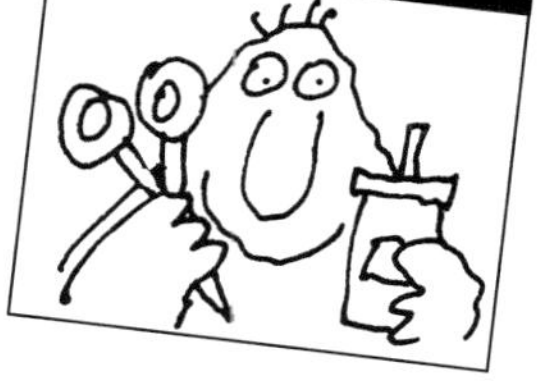

FOCUS WORDS **I like**

Cut out the focus words and paste them in the correct order on the blank lines.

I like

_____ __________.

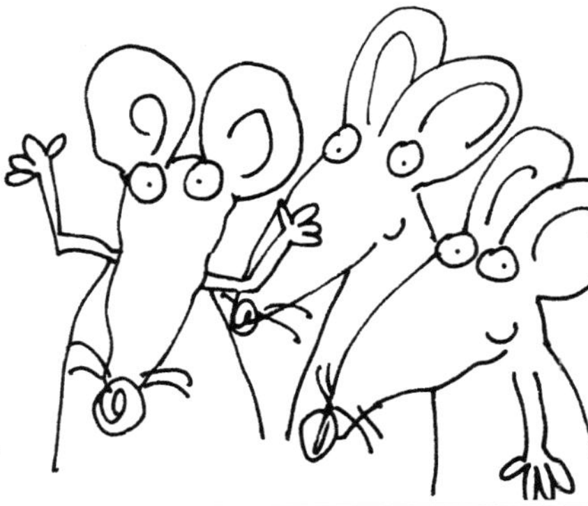

_____ __________.

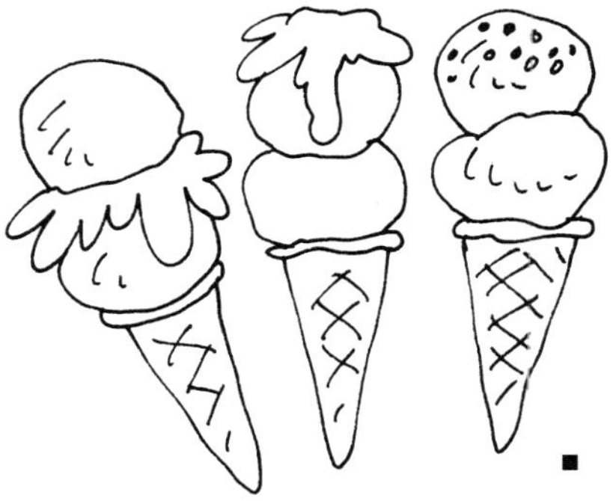

I

like

I

my

to

like

like

I

Titles: I Like Riding • I Like Hats • I Like Red • I Like Elephants

Independent Reinforcement Activity

WRITING

FOCUS WORDS **I like**

Use the focus words to complete the speech bubbles.

I like

____ ________ worms.

____ ________ fish.

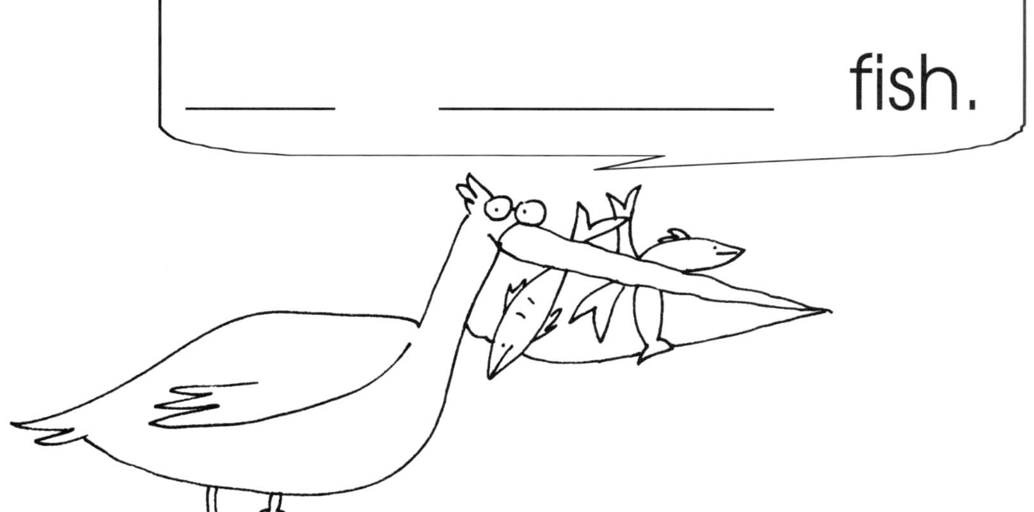

Titles: I Like Riding • I Like Hats • I Like Red • I Like Elephants

Independent Reinforcement Activity

FOCUS WORDS I am

Cut out the focus words and paste them in the speech bubbles in the correct order.

I am

___ ___ cooking.

___ ___ eating.

A I I can am my am

Titles: I Am Jumping • Monkeys • Sailors • I Am Working

Independent Reinforcement Activity

FOCUS WORDS I am

Use the focus words to complete the speech bubbles.

I am

___ ______ Dad.

___ ______ Mom.

___ ______ Baby.

Titles: I Am Jumping • Monkeys • Sailors • I Am Working

Independent Reinforcement Activity

CUTTING and PASTING

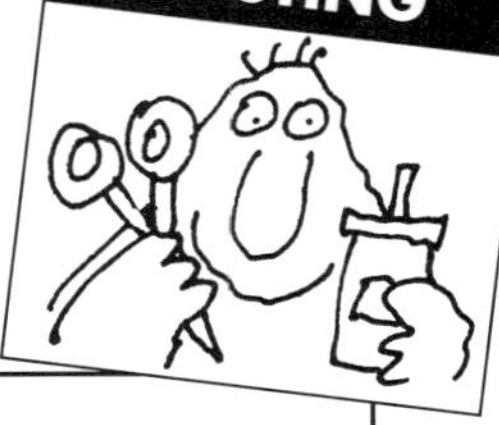

FOCUS WORDS I am a

Cut out the focus words and paste them in their correct order.

I am a

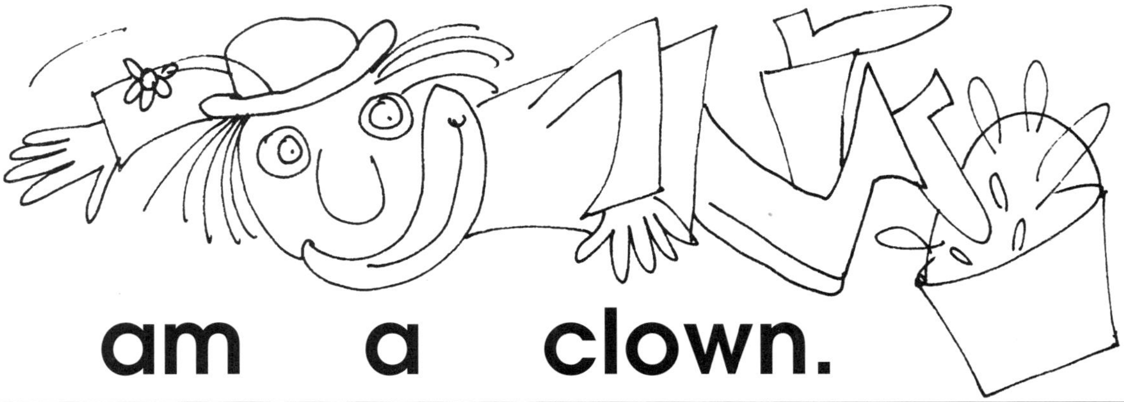

I am a clown.

am

robot. 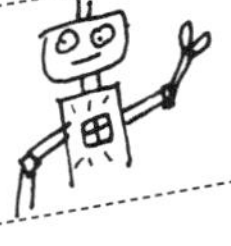

I

a

like

am

clown. 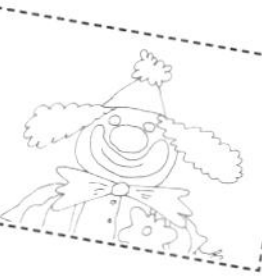

Titles: The Goats • The Family • I Am a Painter • I Am a Bee

Independent Reinforcement Activity

FOCUS WORDS I am a

Use the focus words to complete the rebus sentence.

am I a

________ ________ ________ .

________ ________ ________ .

________ ________ ________ .

Titles: The Goats • The Family • I Am a Painter • I Am a Bee

Independent Reinforcement Activity

FOCUS WORDS Here is a

Cut out the correct words for the caption and paste them in the caption box.

Here is a

a

Here

pig

is

dog

Titles: Here Is a Bird • The Show

Independent Reinforcement Activity

FOCUS WORDS | **Here is the**

Use the focus words to complete the caption.

is the Here

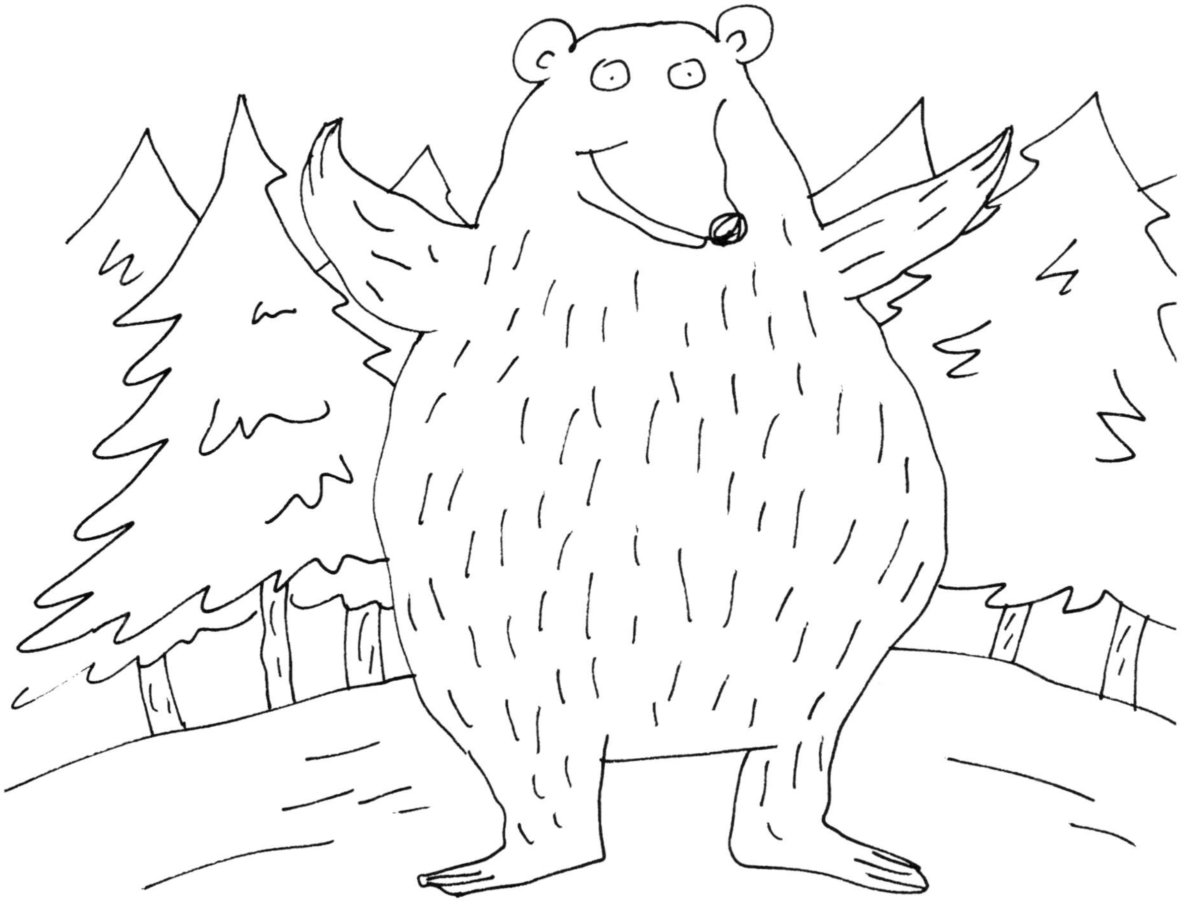

[ ]

monkey bear

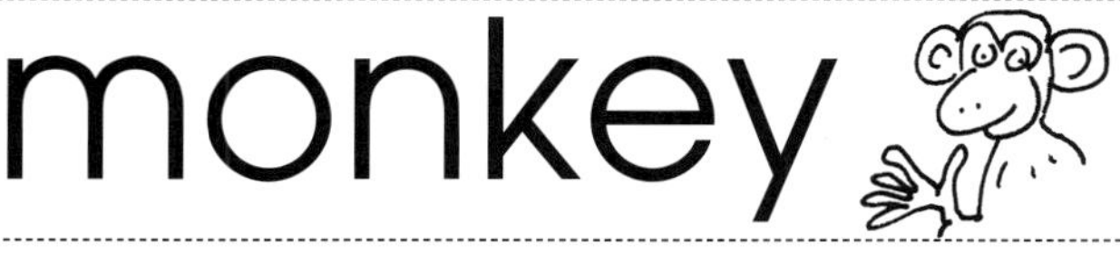

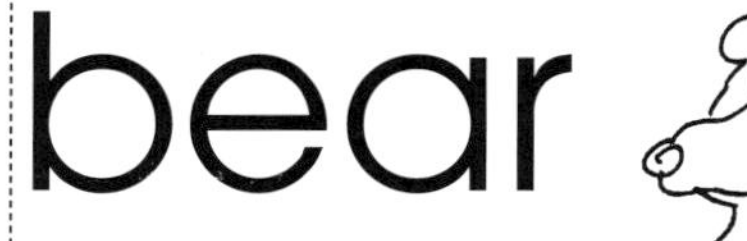

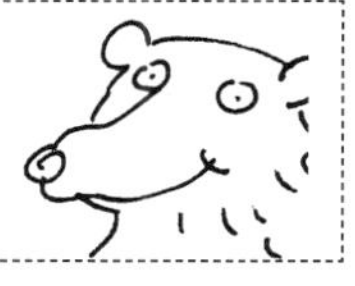

Titles: The Party • The Water Park

Independent Reinforcement Activity

FOCUS WORDS **This is a**

Cut out the correct words for the caption and paste them in the caption box.

This is a

This

a

fish

is

cat

Titles: In the Garden • A Shoe

Independent Reinforcement Activity

FOCUS WORDS This is the

Use the focus words to complete the captions.

is the This

__________ __________ __________ __________.

__________ __________ __________ __________.

Titles: The Hole • The Monster Town

Independent Reinforcement Activity

FOCUS WORDS Look at the

Cut out the words and paste them in the appropriate box to complete the caption.

Look at the

__________ __________ __________ __________

__________ __________ __________ __________

Titles: The Pets • Look at the Robot • Shopping • Look at the Animals

Independent Reinforcement Activity

FOCUS WORDS Look at the

Use the focus words to complete the captions.

at Look the	
______ ______ ______ ______.	______ ______ ______ ______.
 robot	 lion

Titles: The Pets • Look at the Robot • Shopping • Look at the Animals

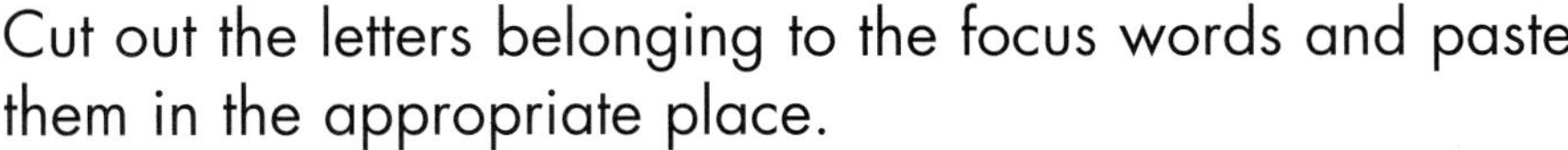

Independent Reinforcement Activity

FOCUS WORDS I can see a

Cut out the letters belonging to the focus words and paste them in the appropriate place.

can	I
______________	______________
see	a
______________	______________

e h c s
l a t n
e t a e

Titles: The Boat • A House

Independent Reinforcement Activity

FOCUS WORDS I can see the

Use the focus words to complete the captions.

I can see the

___ ___ ___ ___ ___ .	___ ___ ___ ___ ___ .
moon	stars

Titles: The Moon • The Balloon Ride

Independent Reinforcement Activity

FOCUS WORDS **I went in the**

Cut out the focus words and paste them under the matching word.

went	I	in
______	______	______
the	went	the
______	______	______

went

is

the

a

the

and

I

went

in

Titles: In the Mud • The Snake

Independent Reinforcement Activity

FOCUS WORDS I went to the

Use the focus words to complete the captions.

I the went to

____ __________

_____ _______ __________.

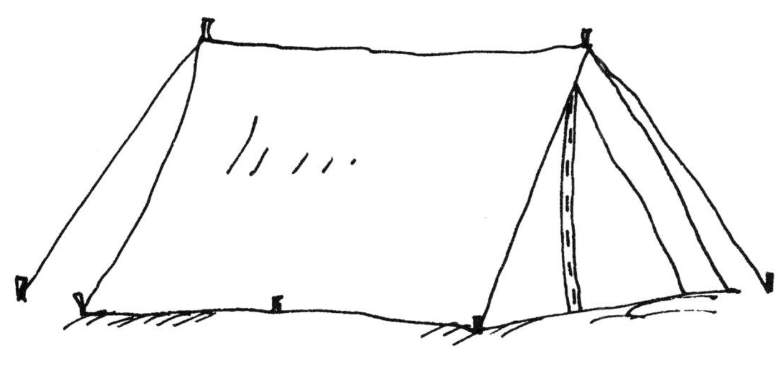

____ __________

_____ _______ __________.

house  tent 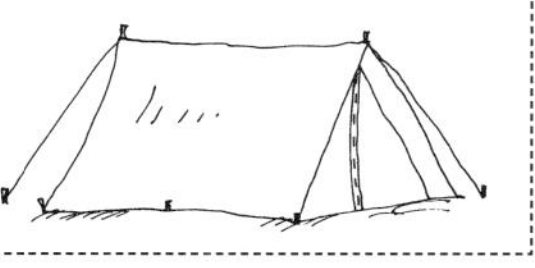

Titles: My Trip • The Bird

Independent Reinforcement Activity

FOCUS WORDS We went in the

Cut out the focus words and paste them in the appropriate box to complete the rebus sentence.

_______ _____________ _______ _____________ .

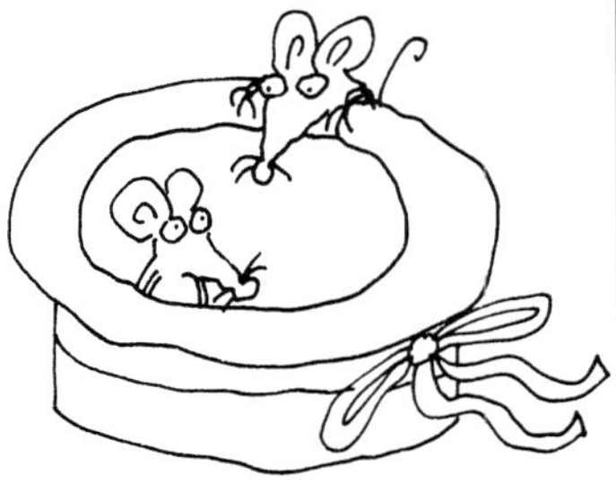

_______ _____________ _______ _____________ .

_______ _____________ _______ _____________ .

the went went in

the We We

in in went We the

Titles: The Mice • The Bears

Independent Reinforcement Activity

FOCUS WORDS We went to the

Use the focus words to complete the captions.

We to went the

____ ________ ____

________ ________.

____ ________ ____

________ ________.

store  pool 

Titles: The Vacation • Our Day

Independent Reinforcement Activity

FOCUS WORDS **I put on my**

Cut out the letters belonging to the focus words and paste them in the appropriate place.

put	on
______________	______________
my	I
______________	______________

e o t l m u c y n p e

Titles: The Race Car • The Snowman

Independent Reinforcement Activity

FOCUS WORDS We put on the

Use the focus words to complete the caption.

We put on the

______ ________ ______ ________

__________ .

hats

shoes

Titles: My Hat • The Spy

Independent Reinforcement Activity

FOCUS WORDS **I like ... and**

Cut out the focus words and paste them in the box with the matching word.

and	like
I	and

my like and I the and

Titles: I Like Jam • Rainbow Town • I Like Boxes • Hats

Independent Reinforcement Activity

FOCUS WORDS I like ... and ...

Use the focus words to complete the captions.

I like and

_______ _______________

____

_______ _______________

____

Titles: I Like Jam • Rainbow Town • I Like Boxes • Hats

Independent Reinforcement Activity

FOCUS WORDS **This is for a**

Cut out the letters belonging to the focus words and paste them on the appropriate line.

this	is
____________	____________
for	**a**
____________	____________

o h s r

t a h i

f s s i t

Titles: The Presents • Dinner

Independent Reinforcement Activity

FOCUS WORDS **This is for the**

Use the focus words to complete the speech bubble.

is the for This

__________ ________ __________

________ ________________.

house car

Titles: Wheels • The New House